Why I wrote "*Financial Planning Solutions: Focusing on Your Finai...*"

Today's around-the-clock financial media machine generates a great deal of "noise". This "noise" can be quite confusing and make it difficult for you to find a consolidated, straight-forward and quality source of financial planning information. This book is meant to be that source of financial planning information for you. By reading this book you will improve your financial planning IQ regardless of if you are a skilled expert or just starting to learn about financial planning. Within *"Financial Planning Solutions: Focusing on Your Financial Success"* you will find:

- Instructions on how you can create your own Financial Plan. These instructions will provide detail on the role wealth management and your investment portfolio will play in your Financial Plan.

- Extensive information on financial planning topics such as education savings, retirement planning, insurance, Social Security, Medicare, Long-term Care and Estate Planning. This information is organized so that you can separately select and read the specific topics applicable to your situation.

- Additional resources and references for all financial planning topics. These resources will direct you to numerous spots that will further your understanding of financial planning.

ABOUT THE AUTHOR

Conor Gillen is the portfolio manager at Carswell Investments, LLC. Conor has spent more than fifteen years helping individual, corporate and non-profit clients achieve their financial goals. Conor graduated from Cornell University in Ithaca, New York. He is a Chartered Financial Analyst (CFA) and Certified Financial Planner (CFP®). Prior to Carswell, Conor worked for over a decade in New York City and London as a restructuring investment banker. Conor resides in Fayetteville, New York with his wife, Tara and three children.

The idea behind his "Financial Planning Solutions" series is to empower the reader by providing useful, accessible, straight-forward material on financial planning. He'd love to hear from you with questions or suggestions (media@cstpublishing.com) as two minds or always better than one.

Inheritance of Hope

Jimmy Albanese Jr. and Conor Gillen have been very close friends since early childhood. In 1994 Jimmy was diagnosed with Non-Hodgkin's Lymphoma and his life along with many family members and friends were changed forever. Stories like Jimmy's below will hopefully become a driving force for other authors to consider donating a portion of their proceeds to a charity that would benefit countless others. This story is an example of how profound love, lifelong friendship and teamwork can result in bringing aid to families in need......

On a chilly day in November of 1994 my life took a dramatic turn that nobody could have ever predicted. What should have been a normal fun-filled bus ride home from school ended up instead becoming a day filled with pain, shock and the beginning of a long road to recovery. I will never forget the feeling of excruciating pain that I felt in my stomach. I knew that something was wrong, but what could it be? In the mind of a seemingly perfectly healthy 14-year-old boy there was nothing that could slow him down or possibly send him to the hospital. After pulling the chord to get off the bus multiple stops prior to my own, I realized that I needed to get help. When my Father showed up at my friend's house he saw me laying on the kitchen floor and knew that time was of the essence.

The next thing I remember is waking up to the bright hospital lights over my bed, my two brothers and parents with tears in their eyes standing next to a team of doctors who had some bad news to deliver. I was told that instead of appendicitis which was the original thought of my surgeon, I actually had a tennis-ball sized tumor pressing on my appendix causing the pain in my stomach to escalate very quickly. The words that followed were words that nobody ever wants to hear, "you have cancer". At any age this type of news sends your mind racing and uncontrollable fear begins to settle in. The three-year journey that followed consisted of endless chemotherapy treatments, radiation and eventually a bone marrow transplant. During those years my mind and body were challenged in ways that I could have never imagined.

Throughout the duration of my battle I was fortunate enough to have an unbreakable support system consisting of family, friends and a medical team who would not take "no" for an answer. There is no doubt in my mind that if it were not for all of these dedicated individuals I would have never survived. The support that my family and I received came to us in many different ways. Things like meals delivered to my house, fundraisers to help my family pay for medical bills, people taking the time to simply listen and endless thoughtful prayers were just a few of the ways that my family and I received assistance.

I have been given a second chance at life and not a day goes by that I do not appreciate this beautiful and rare gift. Although the physical fight may be over for me, the relentless pursuit of finding a cure and supporting others during the course of their own battle continues!

I want to personally thank my very dear friend and author of this exceptional book Conor Gillen for having the courage to do what's right and possessing the compassion to help families during such a difficult time in their lives. His book is not only a great reference for financial guidance but also a shining example of how people can make a difference in this world with a simple act of kindness.

Since beating cancer, Jimmy has been extremely active in helping others battle against the disease. Inheritance of Hope is a 501(c)(3) charity that inspires hope through the unique experiences it brings to young families facing the loss of a parent. A quarter of the proceeds of *"Financial Planning Solutions: Focusing on Your Financial Success"* and all related books will go to Inheritance of Hope. In addition, you can donate directly to this great organization at www.inheritanceofhope.org. Ideally, we would like to inspire other writers to follow the "Learn More. Do Good." motto and tie their publications to charitable giving in some way.

Conor & Jimmy

This book is an evolving document. Help me improve future versions. If you have a topic you want to hear about, a useful financial planning resource or particular question let me know. Contact me at conor@cstpublishing.com.

Copyright © 2018 Center Street Publishing, LLC

All rights reserved. No part of this publication may be reproduced, distributed or transmitted without prior written permission except in the case of brief quotations embodied in reviews and certain other non-commercial uses permitted by copyright law. For permission requests or special discounts on quantity purchases, contact:

Center Street Publishing, LLC
media@cstpublishing.com
208 Center Street
Fayetteville, NY 13066

ISBN 978-1-5323-7584-2 – ePub
ISBN 978-0-692-11839-9 – paperback

A DISCLAIMER:

This publication contains the opinions and ideas of the author and in no way reflects the views of the author's employer, Carswell Investments, LLC. If a reader requires specific advice or services, a competent professional should be consulted. The strategies in this book may not be suitable for every individual and are no guarantee for the production of certain results. This text was written with every effort to provide accurate information, but laws, values and references are all subject to change over time. No warranty is made with respect to the accuracy or completeness contained herein and all parties disclaim any responsibility for the liability, loss or risk incurred as a consequence of the use and application of any of the contents of this book.

CONTENTS

INTRODUCTION

Financial planning is important and somewhere along the line I'm sure you heard that you need to put a formal Financial Plan together. Financial planning can certainly be ignored on a day-to-day basis without much issue, but at some point, you'll have to face certain life events. Your children will want to go to college, the time will come for you to retire or you will need an efficient way to leave assets to those you love when you pass away. These life events can happen without financial planning, but not optimally.

When seeking advice on financial planning, many of us have the same story. You speak with a friend or relative, hop on the internet or even contact a financial professional, but a few weeks or months later you find yourself having accomplished very little (accept maybe incurring some unneeded fees). How you tackle your financial goals is dependent on numerous variables including, age, family structure, and employment. In this book I will address these variables and introduce you to the concrete financial planning and wealth management tools you need to accomplish your goals. In Part I, we will walk through how to put together a formal Financial Plan including how to invest for the long-term. In Part II of the book I'll provide detail on key financial planning topics that might be included in your Financial Plan such as saving for education, retirement, insurance, Social Security, Medicare, Long-term care and estate planning.

For each financial planning topic I've organized the materials by providing answers to the most common questions we encounter in our everyday practice. Every financial planning topic in Part II can be read on a stand-alone basis. This allows you to pick the financial planning topics most applicable to your own unique situation. If you have additional questions on any of these financial planning topics, you can try one of the resources we list at the end of each chapter or contact a financial professional.

Prior to diving into the individual chapters, a "Financial Planning Checklist" is provided to give you an introduction to each financial planning topic. I specifically address different life stages for each checklist item. This is because life stage results in the greatest commonalities when it comes to financial planning. For instance, in your early working years (from age 18 to 45) you are moving into middle age. The focus is typically on family formation, budget construction, the pay-down of debts, the accumulation of assets as well as saving for college expenses and retirement. In our later working years (from age 45 to 65) our lives are moving towards retirement and post-retirement. At this stage in life you should be executing your college and retirement savings plans. In addition, you should increase your understanding of post-retirement issues such as Social Security and Medicare. Finally, in the post-working years (from age 65 on) you will be transitioning from retirement to post-retirement and beyond. You will draw on your retirement savings, use Social Security and form an estate plan to efficiently pass on your assets.

The "Financial Planning Checklist" and the chapters that follow will arm you with the tools you need to construct a Financial Plan and manage it through any life stage. The information provided in this book is not meant to guide every person through every financial issue, but a thorough read will lay the groundwork for you to make much more informed financial decisions.

Financial Planning Checklist

✓ Create a cash flow budget and a net worth statement

In your early working years, creating these documents will allow you to get a good handle on how to set aside an emergency cash fund (a few months of cash reserves) as well as achieve future financial goals such as saving for the purchase of a house or funding college expenses and retirement. As you age, a cash flow budget will include new items such as Social Security and Required Minimum Distributions (RMDs) from your retirement plans.

✓ Make sure your investments match your financial planning goals

Investments can be as simple or as complicated as you would like. Knowledge of the risks and returns of basic investments such as stocks and bonds will be helpful for you even if you have a professional manage assets on your behalf. An investment portfolio should naturally change as you age. It is key to understand your investment timeframe and personal risk tolerance as well as to do your best to limit fees and taxes.

✓ Maximize contributions to your 401(k) and "clean up" your retirement plans

If your employer offers a 401(k) retirement plan, be sure to sign up and contribute at least enough to get your full employer match. This employer match is free money you'll appreciate later in life once the power of compounding returns has kicked in. If you can afford it, contribute the maximum allowed amount to your 401k, which is $18,500 in 2018. In addition, once you reach age 50 you can make an annual "catch-up" contribution to your 401(k). In 2018 this "catch-up" is $6,000.

You may have old 401(k) plans or old Individual Retirement Accounts (IRAs) that you should consolidate for more efficient management and to limit fees. A 401(k) and an IRA are extremely similar. The two accounts serve much of the same purpose in terms of tax deferment. An employer offers a 401(k) retirement plan, while an IRA you own yourself. A 401(k) can easily be "rolled" into your own IRA when you leave an employer or retire.

✓ If you qualify, make a contribution to an Individual Retirement Account (IRA)

You can make pre-tax contributions to a traditional IRA or after-tax contributions to a Roth IRA. Both types of accounts are extremely easy to set up and offer significant tax advantages. Contributions to an IRA are pre-tax and grow tax deferred until you make a withdrawal later in life. Contributions to a Roth IRA are post-tax and you will never be required pay taxes on these funds. In order to make either a tax-deductible contribution to your IRA or any contribution to a Roth IRA your Modified Adjusted Gross Income (Modified AGI) can't exceed certain thresholds. The maximum contributions you can make to either a traditional or Roth IRA in 2018 is $5,500 ($6,500 if you are age 50 or older).

✓ Pay down and avoid high interest rate debt

To the extent you can afford to pay off any type of high interest rate debts, do so. A good rule of thumb is to pay down any debt with a rate higher than a return you think you could realistically receive by putting those same funds in an investment portfolio. For example, if the interest rate you pay on your debt is 6.0% and you think that you can receive a long-term return of 5.5% on invested funds, pay off your outstanding debt.

√ Figure out how much college will cost, then open an account to save for it

Higher education is expensive, but don't put off saving for it even if it's a little bit at a time. Becoming more knowledgeable about the different ways you can save and the financial aid process is key. You can start an account for less than $100 and get tax breaks by saving in a 529 or Coverdell account. You can even receive tax credits just by sending a child to college.

√ Estimate your life insurance needs

Examine the future expenses you may have. Along with ongoing routine/household expenses, you may want life insurance proceeds to fund medical and funeral costs, an outstanding mortgage, or any upcoming education expenses for your children. Understand the different types of insurance policies. Term policies are less expensive than other types of life insurance policies and generally recommended for younger consumers. In addition to term life insurance, you should familiarize yourself with whole life, universal life and variable life insurance policies. Life insurance becomes less important as we age, especially if you have already found other ways to provide for loved ones. You may want to use insurance as a tool to create a certain amount of immediate liquidity when you pass away. These insurance proceeds can fund medical and funeral costs as well as any estate-related expenses.

√ Understand the terms of your other insurance policies

You will find it useful to have a working knowledge of your medical insurance as well as any home insurance or vehicle insurance policies you own. Be sure to review the details on your coverage and the deductibles. Explore obtaining an inexpensive "catch-all" type of insurance policy called an umbrella insurance policy.

√ Create a will

Creating a will can be very straight forward and the creation of a will is essential no matter how basic or extensive your estate planning needs are. If you have a large asset base you may want to explore more complex measures such as creating a trust, but if not, a will should suffice. A will specifies who gets your property when you die and most importantly appoints a personal guardian to raise your children. Later in life, if you have not yet created a will, you should do so. If your children are grown it is not quite as important to appoint a personal guardian to raise your children, but a will still determines who gets certain property when you pass on. It can serve as a sort of "catch-all" where you address any items that may have been left open by the other parts of your estate plan. Typically, a will can be created fairly inexpensively by an estate planning attorney.

√ Execute a living will and powers of attorney

A living will is a legal document you should create in which you state your wishes about life support and other kinds of medical treatment that takes effect if you can't communicate your own wishes. A durable power of attorney for healthcare and finances are legal documents that give another person permission to make medical or financial decisions if you are unable to make these decisions yourself. These documents are extremely accessible, easy to execute, and low cost.

√ Set up your beneficiary designations

Any retirement accounts you have will be passed on to your named beneficiaries at your death. A beneficiary designation is easy to execute if it is not in place already. Naming both a primary beneficiary and alternate beneficiaries will ensure these assets pass to the people you wish and avoid probate. Contact your account custodian (i.e. Fidelity, TD Ameritrade, Schwab etc.) if you are not sure whether your beneficiary designations are in place.

√ Estimate your Social Security benefits

Starting at age 62 you can qualify for retirement benefits. In addition, you may at some point be able to receive either survivor or disability benefits. You can get more information by contacting the Social Security Administration directly to get an estimate of your current benefits. You can contact the Social Security Administration through either their website www.socialsecurity.gov or toll free at 1-800-772-1213.

√ Familiarize yourself with Medicare

Medicare helps citizens 65 and older cover the costs of hospitalization and medical care. You will most certainly deal with Medicare at some point. Medicare has four parts. Medicare Part A covers hospital costs, while Medicare Part B pays some doctors expenses as well as outpatient medical care. Medicare Part C refers to Medicare Advantage Plans which offer identical services as both Medicare Part A and Medicare Part B in addition to offering some extended coverage. Medicare Part D pays for prescription drug costs. To cover the short comings in Medicare coverage you may want to consider Medigap insurance or

Medicare Advantage Plans. You should contact Medicare directly at www.medicare.gov or toll-free at 1-800-Medicare. Your state can provide you with extensive assistance, through your State Health Insurance Assistance Program (SHIP) which you can access at www.shiptacenter.com.

√ Examine Long-Term Care planning

Individuals who require long-term care are generally not sick in the traditional sense, but instead can't perform the basic activities of daily living (ADLs) such as dressing, bathing, eating, toileting, continence and walking. The issue is that this type of care, typically provided by nursing homes and assisted living facilities is not covered by health insurance, Medicare or Medicaid. A long-term care insurance policy can cover these costs in part or in full. Be very careful though as benefit premiums for these policies have been known to rise quickly and benefits have been dropped indiscriminately.

√ Come up with an estate plan

No matter how large or small your asset base, you should construct an estate plan. Estate planning can include different aspects of accounting, financial planning and legal services. Everyone should have at least a simple will and if you have a more complex estate, you may want to examine the use of a trust. Estate plans can become quite complex and you should definitely contact a financial advisor or an estate planning professional with questions that you have.

PART I: MY FINANCIAL PLAN & INVESTMENT PORTFOLIO

Chapter 1: Forming a Financial Plan

✓ Figure out and organize your financial goals and needs. These goals and needs will be dependent on your life stage and can evolve over time.

✓ Construct a Financial Plan that provides detail on how you will best meet your future financial goals and needs. Review this Financial Plan at least annually.

✓ Put together both a Cash Flow Analysis and Net Worth Statement to include in your Financial Plan.

✓ Understand your own tax rate including how both Federal and State income taxes will impact your cash flows.

You should develop a Financial Plan, implement it and maintain it in both good times and bad. You should put your plan in writing as this will help to accomplish both clarity and discipline. Realize that a reliable long-term Financial Plan may not be exciting and developments within the plan may be slow. Your Financial Plan should outline the following:

- Your financial needs
- The timing of these financial needs
- The goals you have for your investments
- The allocation of assets to meet these goals
- An idea of when and how you will maintain the plan (review your plan at least annually and at major life changes)
- A summary of your choices and decisions within the plan

Your Financial Plan will incorporate other topics we cover in detail later in Part II of this book such as your education and retirement savings, insurance, Social Security benefits, Medicare coverage and estate planning. The best way for you to understand a Financial Plan and its creation is probably to review a simplified example of one. You can find numerous examples of online and we provide a very basic sample in this chapter.

What will my Financial Plan look like?

Your Financial Plan can take numerous forms and vary in length. The important thing is that your Financial Plan incorporates the relevant financial information and works for you (can you understand and stick with it?). The sample plan we provide here is not overly complex, but covers a great deal of what you will want to address in your own Financial Plan. Since the Financial Plan we provide is fairly basic, you will want to explore adding elements like a cash flow budget as well as retirement and education funding projections. Many financial advisors use projection tools such as MoneyGuidePro and eMoney or you can try one of the numerous free online projection tools.

Sample Basic Financial Plan

FINANCIAL GOALS:
- Organize various aspects of financial life.
- Establish a formal Financial Plan including educational, retirement and estate planning needs.
- Set time for periodic review of Financial Plan going forward.
- Optimize all investment accounts and review portfolio choices to meet Financial Plan needs and goals.

PLANNING OBJECTIVES:
- Review and organize assets for retirement and determine how resources should be invested to meet both retirement and educational goals.
- Ensure short-term cash goals are met, including upcoming wedding costs of $35,000 and an "Emergency Fund".
- Determine whether home equity line of credit and credit cards should be paid off.

- Review estate planning needs including use of a will and execution of Power of Attorney documents.
- Begin to explore some post-retirement topics such as Social Security and Medicare.

BACKGROUND:

Ben and Judy Graham are 54 and 57 years old, respectively and both are currently employed.

- Ben and Judy have a 21-year-old daughter in her last year of college who they expect to be independent next year and a 15-year-old son who they expect to enroll in college at age 18. They funded their daughter's education expenses through a 529 Plan and expect to have half of their son's college expenses covered by the time he enrolls.

- Ben and Judy's daughter is getting married next year and expenses are estimated to be $35,000.

- In terms of retirement, Ben and Judy want to retire in the same year when he turns 62 and she turns 65. Annual pre-retirement living expenses are assumed to be $170,000 and retirement living expenses are assumed to be $110,000 per year.

- Ben has an Individual Retirement Account (IRA) of roughly $1.4 million and a 401K with his current company worth roughly $400,000. Judy has a 403(b) worth $300,000 and expects to receive a post-tax pension of $20,000 annually. Ben and Judy have $150,000 of cash in a Joint Bank Account.

- It is assumed that maximum plan additions of $18,500 plus a $6,000 "catch-up" (both Ben and Judy are over age 50) will be made each year to both Ben's 401K and Judy's 403(b) until retirement. No IRA contributions will be made because Ben and Judy's joint income phases them out, but Ben and Judy will be able to save an additional $25,000 per year once all of their expenses are covered.

RECOMMENDATIONS / NEXT STEPS:

Emphasis placed on upcoming education expenses and retirement within the next 10 years.

- It appears that Ben and Judy can save $25,000 after tax annually, but a formal cash flow budget should be constructed to provide guidance on future savings and investment. Since retirement is on the horizon, they should sign on to the Social Security website so they can estimate their future benefits as part of the cash flow budget. They should set aside the $35,000 they must pay for their daughter's wedding in a high-yield savings account. The rates on Ben and Judy's home equity line of credit and credit cards are higher than the rate of return they are likely to receive on investments, so cash on hand should be used to pay these off.

- College is Ben and Judy's largest upcoming expense, but it should not be funded at the expense of retirement. As long as they can continue to maximize the contributions to their employer retirement plans, Ben and Judy should fund their son's 529 college account each year. This way, the 529 account can grow tax-deferred and Ben and Judy can receive a state tax deduction annually.

- The year before their son attends college, Ben and Judy should fill out the FAFSA form to see what college expenses can be funded through loans, grants and scholarships. If the rate they have to pay on college loans is more than they think they can receive by investing, they should explore using cash on hand (they have relatively elevated cash levels) in conjunction with the 529 proceeds to pay for college. Once cash needed for college is determined, Ben and Judy can decide how much cash is needed for an "Emergency Fund" and how much remaining cash can be invested.

- It appears Ben and Judy can successfully meet their retirement goals, but they should continue maxing out their contributions to employer retirement plans and run a formal retirement projection analysis to truly analyze the probability of meeting their goals. Once this analysis is performed the asset class weightings of Ben and Judy's investment portfolio will be looked at (Conservative vs. Moderate vs. Aggressive) and a formal Investment Policy Statement (IPS) will be created.

- Ben and Judy have minimal insurance and a calculation should be performed to determine the amount needed to pay off their mortgage and fund expenses during working years up until retirement if either Ben or Judy were to pass away. An affordable term life insurance policy to cover these expenses should be obtained. Post-retirement, it is unlikely that insurance will be needed, but this will be looked at as well.

- Both Ben and Judy have long-term disability policies provided by their employers. They can likely incur the additional cost of further disability insurance they may need, so this will be explored. Ben and Judy don't have an umbrella insurance policy, but should obtain one as they are a relatively inexpensive way to supplement their other policies and protect their net worth.

- Ben and Judy have a will and powers-of-attorney in place, but it is imperative that they review and update their estate documents periodically, especially with large life changes. It does not appear Ben and Judy's asset level is large enough to incur future estate taxes, but they should be aware of these thresholds.

How will my Financial Plan Change?

Once you complete an initial Financial Plan, it will inevitably evolve. Your Financial Plan will change naturally as you age and as life moves forward. We detail these types of changes to your Financial Plan below.

Younger Life: When you are young, you are learning to save as well as the ins and outs of investing. You should develop the discipline to come up with an asset allocation and stick with it. You should participate in any corporate retirement plan available to you and make sure you receive any company match. At this stage, your Financial Plan should focus on forming a cash budget, retirement planning, education savings if you have children, and insurance if needed. Your cash budget may incorporate saving for outflows such as a wedding or first home. As a young investor, you have time and earnings power on your side. This might lead you to believe you should invest aggressively because you have enough time to replace losses. The situation isn't quite that simple though. A young investor may be diligently saving for a large purchase such as a home. These savings may not be appropriate to invest aggressively. In addition, a young investor may not have much cash cushion prior to dipping into funds that should be used for essential expenses. This could lead to a more conservative investment portfolio.

Mid Life: During this "mid-life" period, your career and family life should settle down a bit and you will have more insight into your income and finances. You will be moving towards retirement with a number of productive working years already in the rearview mirror. You may have a few "balls in the air" at this time in your life and cash flow budgeting will be key. You will likely be focused on saving for your children's education. You will make sure to have the correct insurance policies in place to protect your family and have a more detailed idea of how much money it will take for you to retire. To do this, you should estimate your future living expenses, the value of future income streams (pensions, social security etc.) and your investment portfolio's potential returns. This is the point in life when you will hopefully reach a higher level of income, so tax planning will become more of a concern. Usually investors during this time period will use a more aggressive or moderately aggressive portfolio to grow wealth.

Transitioning/Evolving Retirees: This period is typically marked by peak earnings and savings years. Ideally at this stage in life, your household expenses will have stabilized and any children you have should hopefully be self-sufficient. There is no official pre-retirement period, but during such a time you'll start trying to address questions such as; When do I retire? Do I have enough money to retire? How much can I afford to withdraw annually to fund my retirement? Your focus should be on a cash flow budget that incorporates these variables. You should familiarize yourself with Social Security, Medicare and estate planning. You should figure out the most tax efficient way to withdraw funds in retirement. Worries about retirement can cause conservatism as you convert your portfolio from an accumulation phase to a distribution phase. In terms of asset allocation, safety of principal will become increasingly important, but your assets may continue to need growth because you still have many years to live.

Mature Retirees: At this point in life you should get your financial house in order. You may want to make sure someone else has an understanding of your investment accounts, insurance documents and estate plan including knowing the location of all relevant documents and contact information of all professionals you work with (accountant, lawyer, financial advisor). Your cash budgeting should focus on how you meet ongoing needs, and estate planning should be front and center. You should consolidate your financial accounts as much as possible for simplicity. Health and healthcare costs may become more of a factor in your life. Your asset allocation during this period can take a number of forms. If you need all of your assets for living expenses your asset allocation may be more conservative. If your asset base is sufficient to cover all your expenses and you plan to provide assets to heirs, you may want to have a more aggressive portfolio to better match the age of any heirs.

How do I best construct and analyze a Cash Flow Budget?

One of the most important aspects of forming a Financial Plan is constructing some sort of cash flow budget. We provide you with a sample cash flow budget template as well as an explanation of what goes into a cash flow budget in this chapter. A cash flow budget can take numerous forms. So long as it is accurate, you can use whatever format makes you most comfortable. A cash flow budget is important in helping you to manage your liquidity and make financial decisions, such as how much of your cash to put in an investment portfolio and the most efficient way to save for college.

A cash flow budget compares your cash inflows to your expenses. You should try to compare inflows and expenses on a cash basis to get the most accurately timed projections. Your inflows will not simply consist of wages, but can include other items such as investment income, gifts from 3rd parties, pension benefits, Social Security and partnership income.

Your expenses may be a bit more complex than your cash inflows and it is a good idea to obtain a year or more of detail on your expenses through bank and credit card statements. Certain expenses can be fixed in nature such as your mortgage. Other expenses are more variable or even one-time such as money spent on a vacation. When you have a good idea of your cash inflows and expenses you should project them and make sure the timing of the receipts and disbursements is correct. Once you have your cash flow budget, you can begin to compare your projections to your actual cash inflows and expenses to get a handle on the variance between the two. Below is a sample cash flow budget. Note that you will likely want to project your inflows and outflows for at least one year.

Cash Flow Budget						
	Jan	Feb	Mar	Apr	May	Jun
Monthly Inflow						
Monthly Salary	$10,000	$10,000	$10,000	$10,000	$10,000	$10,000
Total Monthly Inflow	**$10,000**	**$10,000**	**$10,000**	**$10,000**	**$10,000**	**$10,000**
Monthly Expenses						
Groceries	(1,000)	(1,000)	(1,000)	(1,000)	(1,000)	(1,000)
Hobbies /Recreation	(500)	(500)	(500)	(500)	(500)	(500)
Insurance	(250)	(250)	(250)	(250)	(250)	(250)
Exercise/Gym	(200)	(200)	(200)	(200)	(200)	(200)
Verizon	(75)	(75)	(75)	(75)	(75)	(75)
Mortgage	(1,500)	(1,500)	(1,500)	(1,500)	(1,500)	(1,500)
Miscellaneous	(1,915)	(1,915)	(1,915)	(1,915)	(1,915)	(1,915)
Total Expenses	**($5,440)**	**($5,440)**	**($5,440)**	**($5,440)**	**($5,440)**	**($5,440)**
Net Cash Flow	**$4,560**	**$4,560**	**$4,560**	**$4,560**	**$4,560**	**$4,560**
Cumulative Cash Flow	**$4,560**	**$9,120**	**$13,680**	**$18,240**	**$22,800**	**$27,360**
Beginning Cash Balance	$25,000	$29,560	$34,120	$38,680	$43,240	$47,800
Net Cash Flow	$4,560	$4,560	$4,560	$4,560	$4,560	$4,560
Ending Cash Balance	**$29,560**	**$34,120**	**$38,680**	**$43,240**	**$47,800**	**$52,360**
Cash for College	**$4,560**	**$9,120**	**$13,680**	**$18,240**	**$22,800**	**$27,360**

How do I best construct and analyze a Net Worth Statement?

Are you thinking of buying a home, opening a business, or taking out a loan? These and basically any other financial actions you take will impact your Net Worth Statement which compares your assets to your liabilities (assets – liabilities = net worth). If your assets exceed your liabilities, you will have a positive net worth. If your assets are less than your liabilities, you will have a negative net worth. Your assets and liabilities can be short-term or long-term in nature. Some examples of short-term assets and liabilities as well as long-term assets and liabilities are shown in our sample Net Worth Statement.

Net Worth Statement	
Assets	
Bank Accounts	$6,000
House	$400,000
Car	$30,000
Total Assets	**$436,000**
Liabilities	
Mortgage	300,000
Car Loan	20,000
Total Liabilities	**$320,000**
Equity (Assets - Liabilities)	**$116,000**

How do I calculate my taxable income?

A key part of forming your financial plan is understanding your taxes. Regardless of if you use a tax professional or financial advisor to help you with your tax filing, it is a good idea to have a working knowledge of how taxes and your tax rate will impact your financial planning. We help you understand the basics of your income taxes, but if you have further questions on your taxes, always be sure to ask a tax professional, especially given the changes brought about by the recent Tax Cuts and Jobs Act of 2017.

Your taxable income is the amount of income remaining after you have made all appropriate exemptions, exclusions and deductions from your gross income. This tax calculation is detailed annually on your IRS Form 1040. Note that there are many complexities to calculating your taxes and this information is meant strictly to provide you with high level guidance. The general tax formula is provided here. Further detail on the General Tax Equation is contained in Appendix A of this book.

General Income Tax Equation
Income (broadly conceived)
Less: Exclusions from Gross Income
Gross Income
Less: Deductions for Adjusted Gross Income (AGI)
Adjusted Gross Income
Less: Greater of (i) Itemized Deductions or (ii) Standard Deduction
Less: Personal and dependency exemptions
Taxable Income

Source: Internal Revenue Service (IRS)

What is my federal income tax rate?

The exhibit below shows the federal tax brackets that apply to your taxable income. Once you calculate your taxable income (see the General Income Tax Equation), you can estimate your federal tax rate. As shown in the exhibit, the amount of your taxable income subject to a particular federal tax rate depends on the type of tax filer you are.

Marginal Tax Rates for 2017

Marginal Tax Rate	Single Filer	Married Filing Jointly or Qualified Widower	Married Filing Seperately	Head of Household
10%	$0 - $9,325	$0 - $18,650	$0 - $9,325	$0 - $13,350
15%	$9,326 - $37,950	$18,651 - $75,900	$9,326 - $37,950	$13,351 - $50,800
25%	$37,951 - $91,900	$75,901 - $153,100	$37,951 - $76,550	$50,801 - $131,200
28%	$91,901 - $191,650	$153,101 - $233,350	$76,551 - $116,675	$131,201 - $212,500
33%	$191,651 - $416,700	$233,351 - $416,700	$116,676 - $208,350	$212,501 - $416,700
35%	$416,701 - $418,400	$416,701 - $470,700	$208,351 - $235,350	$416,701 - $444,550
39.6%	$418,401+	$470,701+	$235,351+	$444,551+

Source: Internal Revenue Service (IRS)

In December of 2017 the President signed into law the Tax Cuts and Jobs Act of 2017. The Act adjusted the tax brackets beginning in 2018. These new brackets will be in place through 2025. If they are not renewed, after 2025 the tax brackets will shift back to 2017 levels.

Marginal Tax Rates for 2018

Marginal Tax Rate	Single Filer	Married Filing Jointly or Qualified Widower	Married Filing Seperately	Head of Household
10%	$0 - $9,525	$0 - $19,050	$0 - $9,525	$0 - $13,600
12%	$9,526 - $38,700	$19,051 - $77,400	$9,526 - $38,700	$13,601 - $51,800
22%	$38,701 - $82,500	$77,401 - $165,000	$38,701 - $82,500	$51,801 - $82,500
24%	$82,501 - $157,500	$165,001 - $315,000	$82,501 - $157,500	$82,501 - $157,500
32%	$157,501 - $200,000	$315,001 - $400,000	$157,501 - $200,000	$157,501 - $200,000
35%	$200,001 - $500,000	$400,001 - $600,000	$200,001 - $300,000	$200,001 - $500,000
37%	$500,001 +	$600,001 +	$300,001 +	500,001 +

Source: Internal Revenue Service (IRS)

You will pay tax at a given tax bracket only for each dollar of taxable income within that bracket. This gives rise to your Effective Tax Rate. This is probably best seen through an example. For simplicity, let's use the 2017 tax brackets and assume a single taxpayer, with $40,000 of gross income and no children. The taxpayer is under 65, is not blind and takes the standard deduction.

- First let's calculate the taxpayer's taxable income: $40,000 gross income - $6,500 standard deduction - $4,150 personal exemption = $29,350 of taxable income. Note the Tax Cuts and Jobs Act of 2017 changed personal exemptions and deductions as well as the Federal tax brackets starting in 2018. Much more information on deductions and exemptions are contained in Appendix A of this book.

- Next let's calculate taxation of the first tax bracket. Since the taxpayer's taxable income is larger than the upper threshold of the first tax bracket of 10%, they will be taxed on each dollar in the bracket as follows ($9,325 - $0) = $9,325. Applying the 10% marginal tax rate results in $932.50 of tax. The taxation of the second tax bracket is a bit different than the first since the taxpayer's taxable income is smaller than the upper threshold of the second tax bracket. This means the taxable income is ($29,350 - $9,325) = $20,025. Applying the 15% marginal tax rate results in $3,003.75 of tax.

- The total tax of $932.50 from the 10% tax bracket plus the $3,003.75 of tax from the second tax bracket results in $3,936.25 of federal tax. This means your Effective Tax Rate is actually $3,936.25 / $40,000 of gross income or roughly 9.84%. The Marginal Tax Rate is the tax you will pay on one additional dollar of income. In this case the marginal tax rate is 15%.

Quick Tip: *State taxes, for example New York State taxes are applied in an extremely similar manner but are lower than Federal taxes. You can walk through New York State tax rates and their application at https://www.tax.ny.gov/.*

Further Resources

- **www.irs.gov** – this is the official website of the Internal Revenue Service (IRS). It contains all sorts of information that will impact your Financial Plan. Although the information can be a bit dry, the IRS website can provide answers to almost any tax and many financial planning questions.

- **www.bankrate.com** – a good deal of data on personal finances to help you create a budget, prior to retirement or in retirement. The website has useful resources on taxes as well.

- **www.turbotax.com** – although most people use turbo tax as a tool to file their own tax returns, the website has grown to include useful explanations on all parts of your taxes. Explanations and examples are more user-friendly than those on the IRS website.

Note: Numerous websites (Morningstar, Kiplinger etc.) will help with financial planning, but may require at least some degree of membership.

Books:

Nissenbaum, Martin et al. *Ernst & Young Financial Planning Guide*. John Wiley & Sons, Inc., 2004.

Helps you form a plan that allows you to reduce taxes, aids you in understanding your investments and helps you correctly manage your money. Explanations in this book will be key to helping you create your own Cash Flow Budget. Make sure to incorporate updates since publication.

Hallman, G. Victor and Rosenbloom, Jerry S. *Personal Financial Planning: Seventh Edition.* **McGraw-Hill Companies, Inc., 2003.**

Pulls together a large number of financial planning topics (education expenses, retirement etc.) and provides explanations of how they work together in the formation of an in-depth Financial Plan and your own Cash Flow Budget.

Chapter 2: Wealth Management & My Investment Portfolio

✓ Understand the risk and return characteristics of the various asset classes including equities (stocks), fixed income (bonds) and cash.

✓ Derive an Investment Policy Statement (IPS) and investment portfolio that best allows you to meet the goals outlined in your Financial Plan.

✓ Decide if you want to use active or passive investments as well as if you want to use a financial professional to help manage your assets.

✓ As time goes on, rebalance your investment portfolio to make sure that your asset allocation remains consistent with your financial goals.

The new millennium has been challenging for investors and marked by volatility. More than ever, investors are questioning the make-up of their portfolios and the advice they receive. There is no investing magic bullet and trying to out-guess the financial markets is not a recipe for success. As we detail in this book, your best course of action is developing a long-term Financial Plan. Your Financial Plan will include an Investment Policy Statement (IPS). This IPS will dictate the holdings in your diversified investment portfolio and provide discipline and guidance for all your future investing.

In this chapter, we will look at how to construct and manage an investment portfolio to best meet the needs and goals outlined in your Financial Plan. We will examine the different available asset classes and their characteristics. We'll explain why your investment portfolio should spread risk by diversifying across many different asset classes while keeping expenses low and limiting taxes. Investing across multiple asset classes reduces the inherent risk of being invested in just a single stock or bond, but no investment strategy can protect your portfolio all the time. You must be prepared for poor months, quarters and years. In fact, a portfolio consisting of 50% stocks and 50% bonds will experience losses on average roughly once every five years. These periods of poor performance can make it difficult for you to follow your investment strategy.

Should I manage my own investment portfolio?

One of the first decisions you will make (but that you can always revisit) is whether to manage your own portfolio or to use a financial professional. It is possible to manage your own portfolio (and probably better than using just any unqualified, expensive advisor), but it is difficult. To put together a properly diversified portfolio that limits fees and taxes you must have the right combination of time, knowledge, analytical tools and discipline. The difficulties individual investors have when it comes to managing their own portfolios are clearly shown in a study by DALBAR, a financial research firm that focuses on investor behavior.

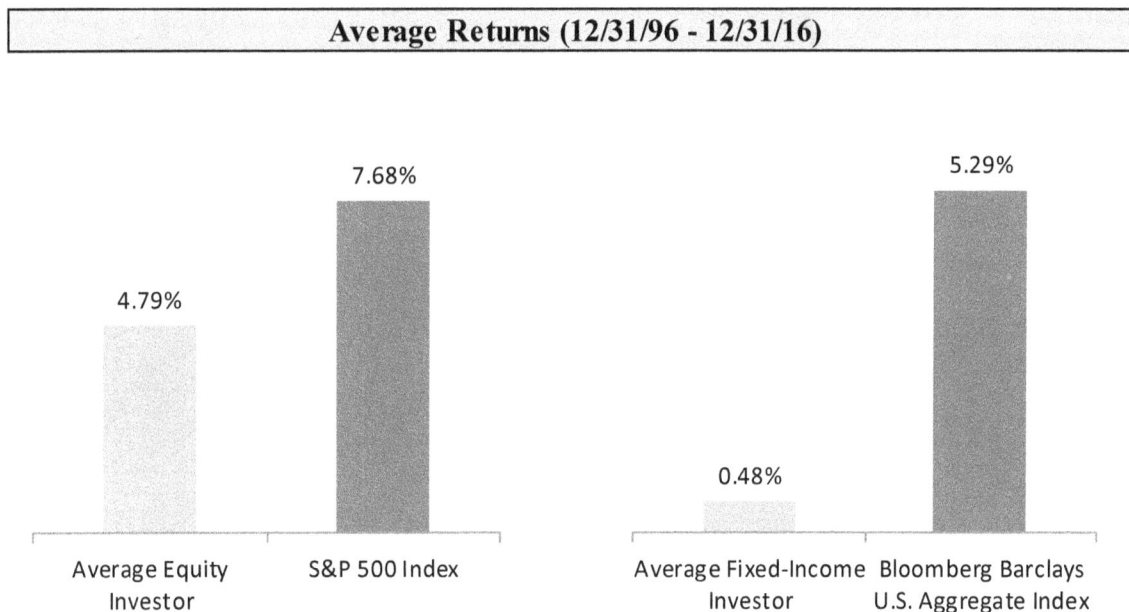

Average Returns (12/31/96 - 12/31/16)

4.79%	7.68%
Average Equity Investor	S&P 500 Index

0.48%	5.29%
Average Fixed-Income Investor	Bloomberg Barclays U.S. Aggregate Index

Source: DALBAR. Returns for average equity and fixed-income investors calculated by DALBAR. DALBAR uses data from the Investment Company Institute (ICI), Standard & Poor's, Bloomberg Barclays Indices and proprietary sources to compare mutual fund investor returns to an appropriate set of benchmarks. The study utilizes mutual fund sales, redemptions and exchanges each month as the measure of investor behavior. These behaviors reflect the "average investor." Based on this behavior, the analysis calculates the "average investor return" for various periods. These results are then compared to the returns of respective indexes. Ending values for the indexes and hypothetical equity and fixed-income investor investments are based on average annual total returns.

Yes, you might be able to successfully invest yourself, but as the DALBAR study shows, more often than not, individual investors fall into the common emotional traps of overconfidence, fear of regret and following the investment pack. A qualified financial advisor can bring discipline and clarity to the investment process for you, helping to avoid these emotional traps. If you do choose to rely on a financial professional, be sure to use an independent, fee-only financial advisor as opposed to a registered representative or broker. The reason for this is imbedded in the legal standards of the Investment Advisers Act of 1940. The Act requires anyone who offers investment advice for a flat or asset-based fee to register as an investment advisor. According to the law, advisors must disclose any conflicts of interest and always act in the best interest of clients (act as a fiduciary). Registered representatives and brokers are not held to these same standards and most troubling are often paid by parties other than you, the investor.

Quick Tip: *make sure any financial professional uses a third-party custodian (Fidelity, Charles Schwab etc.) and an account in your own name. Under no circumstances should an advisor take custody of your assets. This is how many investment scandals have occurred.*

Should I use active or passive investing?

Another investing decision you'll have to make when it comes to your portfolio is whether you should use active or passive investment management (although the decision is not necessarily mutually exclusive). Active investing, most commonly in the form of mutual funds, attempts to out-perform either the market or a benchmark through a variety of techniques that typically include some sort of stock picking and/or market timing. Passive investing is based on the belief that markets are efficient and extremely difficult to beat, especially after taking into consideration fees and taxes. Passive managers try to deliver market returns while limiting turnover and expenses. Exchange traded funds (ETFs) have become extremely popular with passive managers due to their liquidity, tax efficiency, trading flexibility and ability to mimic indexes such as the S&P 500.

When debating the use of active or passive management, you should be aware that financial media (television, magazines etc.) has a vested interest in making you believe that portfolio success is entirely dependent on active management methods such as (1) getting in and out of the market at the right time (2) picking individual securities correctly, or (3) discovering the next all-star fund or manager. If the media can convince you of this, you will purchase another magazine or tune in to another television program providing investment "expertise" or suggestions. Contrary to the messages from the financial media though, research has shown that the active management methodologies above actually have a negative contribution to the total return level of a diversified portfolio.[1]

---

(1) Xiong, J.X., Ibbotson, R.G., and Chen, P. 2010. "The Equal Importance of Asset Allocation and Active Management". Financial Analyst's Journal, March/April.

Yes, there are active managers that experience periods of outperformance, but before deciding to use active management as an integral part of your portfolio you should consider:

- It is easy to find top-performing funds after the fact, but there is little evidence that past investing success is an indicator of future success. The Wall Street Journal conducted an extensive study that concluded only 14% of the funds rated 5 stars by the popular ratings agency Morningstar in 2004 carried the same rating in 2014.

- Actively managed funds very often underperform their applicable benchmarks. According to SPIVA® Statistics and Reports produced by S&P Dow Jones, 88.3% of actively managed Large-cap Funds underperformed the S&P 500 for the five-year period ending December 31, 2016. This is consistent for many other asset classes.

- A key reason it is extremely difficult to time financial markets is because financial markets tend experience large gains that are concentrated over a relatively small number of trading days. As shown in the following exhibit, during the past 20 years if you missed the 20 best trading days the return on the S&P 500 was 1.67% and if you missed the 30 best trading days during this time period the return was negative.

Growth of the S&P 500 (12/31/96 - 12/31/16)

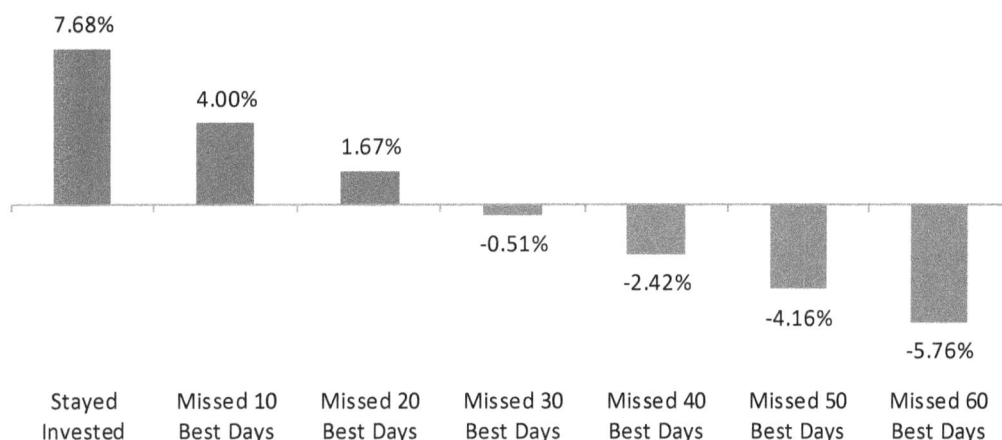

Source: J.P. Morgan Asset Management analysis using data from Bloomberg. Returns are based on the S&P 500 Total Return Index, an unmanaged, capitalization-weighted index that measures the performance of 500 large capitalization domestic stocks representing all major industries. Past performance is not indicative of future returns. An individual cannot invest directly in an index. Data as of December 30, 2016.

- Active managers often have elevated levels of cash as they wait to time the market or find a hot investment. Cash has a much lower level of return versus other asset classes over time, so active managers can end up with "cash drag" hurting portfolio performance.

- Active managers can experience "style drift" as they attempt to beat the market. For example, an investor in an actively managed domestic large-cap fund can suddenly find their fund with more foreign holdings than expected.

- Active management is expensive compared to passive management due to (i) higher management fees which occur because active funds must pay for things like research, marketing and sales teams (ii) increased holding turnover that drives up fees and commissions and (iii) greater tax exposure due to accelerated capital gains from more aggressive trading. The exhibit below shows an example of how big a difference elevated active management fees can make over long periods of time. A difference of just less than 1.0% in fees

43

over 30 years can make a difference approaching $1.0 million in the value of
your portfolio.

Total Fees on $1 million Investment - 30 Years

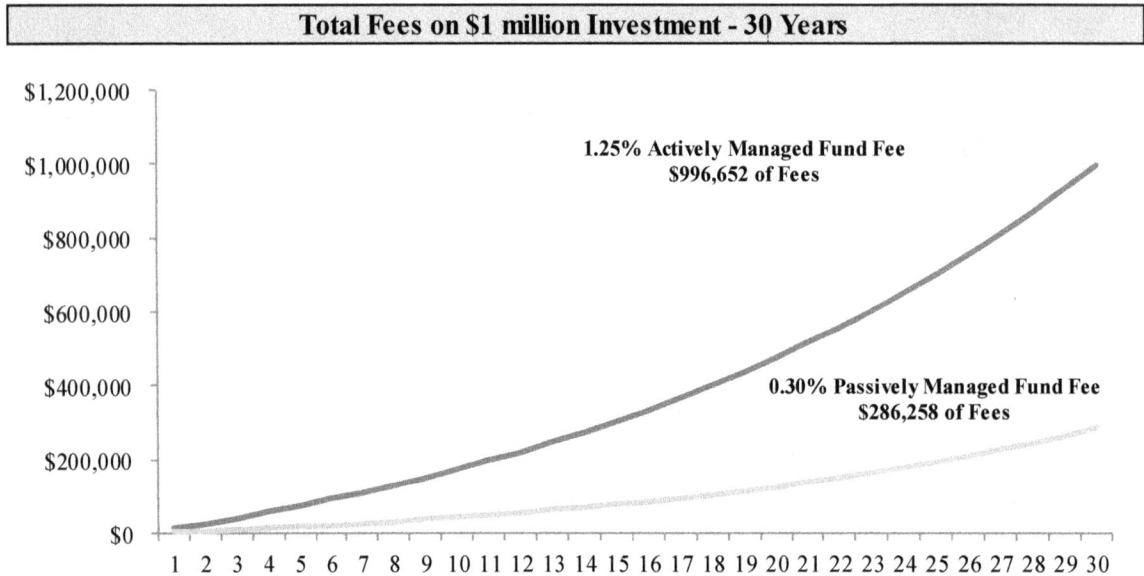

1.25% Actively Managed Fund Fee
$996,652 of Fees

0.30% Passively Managed Fund Fee
$286,258 of Fees

Exhibit assumes a beginning portfolio value of $1 million with a 7% annual return.

Quick Tip: you can find out much more about Exchange Traded Funds (ETFs)

in the "ETF University" section of the etf.com website http://www.etf.com/etf-

education-ce.html.

What is asset allocation and how does it relate to my Financial Plan?

Once you have decided whether to manage your own portfolio and if active or passive management should be used, it is time to invest. Asset allocation at its core is a type of investing that divides wealth into different categories such as stocks, bonds, real estate, cash and alternative assets to reduce the risk of large loss. Asset allocation should be the guiding principal for the investment portion of your Financial Plan. The amount of money you commit to each asset class is the most important factor in determining the growth path your money will take as well as your portfolio risk. For instance, an over-weighting of stocks as opposed to bonds could generate greater returns over time, but result in greater risk as well.

Numerous academic studies point to asset allocation as the main determinant of portfolio returns, as detailed in the exhibit below.

Drivers of Portfolio Return

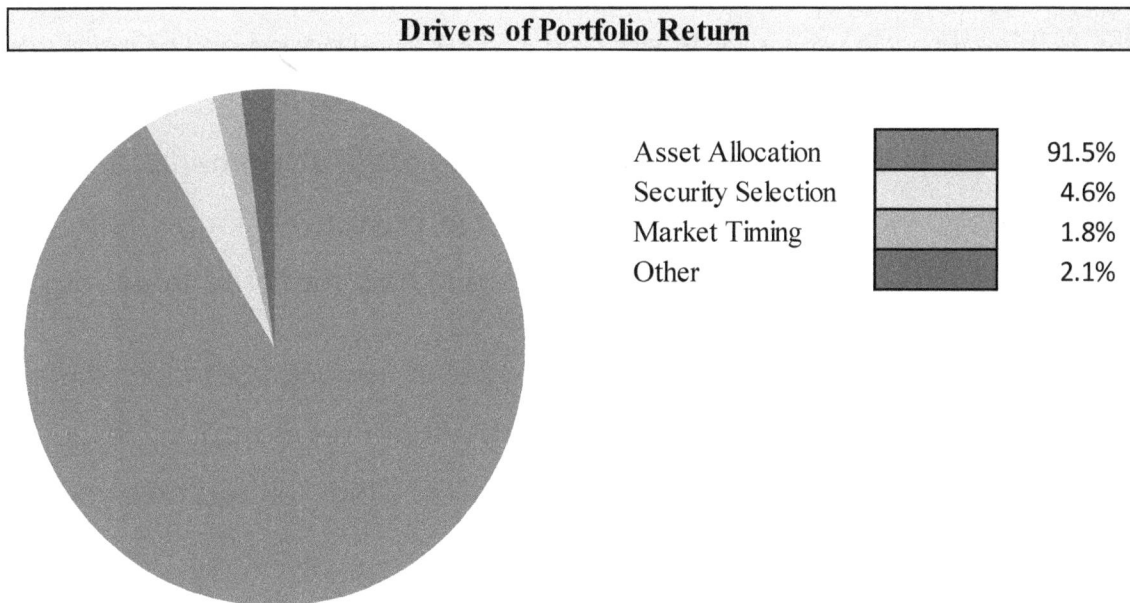

Asset Allocation	91.5%
Security Selection	4.6%
Market Timing	1.8%
Other	2.1%

Source: "Determinants of Portfolio Performance II: An Update" by Gary P. Brinson, Brian D. Singer and Gilbert L. Beebower, Financial Analysts Journal May/June 1991.

This is contrary to the belief that you or a professional asset manager can select superior securities or time markets. Your investment portfolio and asset allocation will be unique. It will be based on your financial needs today and in the future. The funding of future liabilities such as college expenses or retirement is a typical goal for your investment portfolio and asset allocation. You should consider not only the wealth you have invested in public instruments such as stocks and bonds, but the wealth you can attribute to other assets such as real estate, interests in a business, pension income and social security.

Investing in multiple asset classes can help increase your portfolio returns while taking less overall risk because of the unique risks of the different asset classes (bond performing well when stocks perform poorly and vice versa). You should select an asset allocation mix that best fits your short-term and long-term financial needs. Once you have selected your asset allocation, you should pick the investments that best represent each asset class. We thoroughly review these investments in this chapter, but you should do your own research and make sure each investment matches your needs. The four steps of asset allocation include:

1. Think through your investment portfolio risk level based on financial goals. Translate this into asset classes. Asset classes are broad categories of investments such as stocks, bonds, alternative investments and cash. Generally, more risky stock investments are paired with longer-term goals, while less risky bond investments are used to help meet shorter-term goals.

2. Familiarize yourself with and analyze the individual asset classes (stocks, bonds, alternative assets etc.). Select asset classes based on unique risk, expected return, correlation and tax efficiency that will best help you meet your financial goals.

3. Choose securities to best represent each asset class. Make sure the securities are tax efficient, low-cost and have little tracking error. Tracking error is the divergence between the price behavior of a security or a

portfolio and the price behavior of a benchmark. Look for transparency and high liquidity.

4. Implement your strategy and rebalance your investment portfolio as appropriate. Rebalancing a portfolio is a counterintuitive process in which you sell asset classes when the value of the asset class rises and buy asset classes when the value of the asset class falls. You should rebalance your portfolio periodically to keep your investments in line with your tolerance for risk. The portfolio rebalancing process requires discipline and can be difficult to execute.

Asset allocation decisions are not permanent. In addition to the natural changes in your Financial Plan that will occur with age, other life changes can lead to modifications of your Financial Plan. These life changes can include health developments, spending habits, lifestyle decisions and portfolio performance. You should not make knee-jerk changes to your Financial Plan or investment portfolio, but a few good reasons to make a change include:

- Your financial goals are within reach – a strong market performance increases the value of your assets beyond your expectations which may cause you to make changes to your Financial Plan.
- You realize you will not need all your assets – if you have assets sufficient to cover all of your estimated needs, you may shift your thinking and financial planning to how you help future generations.
- Your risk tolerance shifts – your appetite for risk and holding risky assets in your portfolio may diminish as you approach retirement.

Quick Tip: Vanguard has a very informative White Paper titled "Best Practices for Portfolio Rebalancing" that explains the rebalancing process.

How should I view investment risk?

Investment risk is not completely straight forward. There is inherent risk in financial markets, but what happens outside the markets in your everyday life can impact how you view risk too. Your job security, family matters and health, among other factors will impact your tolerance for risk. When thinking about your Financial Plan, you should understand not only the risk characteristics of various investments and financial markets, but the risks in your personal life as well.

The returns you receive on your investments are always related to risk. If you take little risk then you should expect little return and large risk taking should be rewarded with large returns. Views on risk can vary. Some see risk as simply losing money and others see risk as volatility. Volatility as a financial measure refers to the uncertainty about the size of the changes in a security or asset's value. Higher volatility means that values can potentially be spread out over a larger range and the price of the security can change dramatically over a short time period either positively or negatively. A lower volatility means that a security's value does not fluctuate dramatically, but changes at a steadier pace. The measure of volatility requires a period of time, be it minutes, days, weeks or years. In general, the longer the time period, the lower the level of volatility.

Of the two major asset classes, equities (stocks), for which returns are dependent on dividends and earnings growth, have a higher long-term expected return because there is greater volatility (risk) to these returns. Fixed income (bonds) which pay interest periodically and their principal at maturity provide lower returns and are generally less volatile than equities.

Despite the mountains of financial questionnaires that will claim to pinpoint your risk tolerance for the purposes of creating a Financial Plan, risk and risk tolerance are tough to interpret and almost impossible to quantify. Although it is not a perfect science, when trying to pin down your risk tolerance, you should think about the following concepts:

- People tend to be more optimistic about stocks after the market goes up and more pessimistic after the market goes down.
- Too much weight is given to recent market information and too little weight is given to long-term fundamentals.
- Overconfidence leads to excess trading, elevated fees and ultimately underperformance.
- Your actual tolerance for risk is typically less than your stated tolerance for risk.
- What is the maximum value your current portfolio has lost in the past? Can you tolerate such a loss?

Volatility can cause you to abandon a well-thought out investment plan at very inopportune times. When considering your own risk tolerance, you should be aware of how widely investment performance can vary even within a single year.

- Consider 1987, the year of "Black Monday" when stocks fell over 30% within a few day period in October. Stocks, as represented by the S&P 500 had risen 36% prior to the events of Black Monday and actually ended the year with a gain of 5.1%. Most investors only recall the losses incurred on "Black Monday" without mentioning the fact that the stock market ended that year with gains.

In gauging your risk tolerance, you should reflect on your feelings and actions during bear markets or think about how you would react during your current portfolio's worst periods of past performance. Although staying with your Financial Plan when it loses money can be extremely frustrating at times, you can't predict the sudden shifts in market returns. Missing out on large market recoveries or even a few days of gains can severely hurt your portfolios returns as we discussed previously.

What are the characteristics of the equity asset class?

Equities (stocks) and fixed income (bonds) are fundamentally different investments. They have different obligations to owners, provide different income streams and are taxed differently. Owning stocks means you own part of a company and are entitled to a fair share of profits through dividends and share price appreciation. If you own stocks you have earnings risk and the value of the stock you own is likely to fall if future earnings decline. If you own a stock, you are the last to receive any value in the event of a company's liquidation.

U.S. Equities

The U.S. diversified stock market should be a cornerstone of any portfolio that desires growth. There are several indexes and funds that can be used to represent this market. In the long run, equity markets have been one of the few asset classes to generate returns greater than inflation. U.S. stocks have delivered strong long-term returns despite wars, recessions and financial collapses. You should be aware however, that for periods as long as a decade, U.S. equities have generated low or even negative returns.

The U.S. equity market can be broken down into quite a few styles and sectors. There are many low-cost investment vehicles that provide access to these various styles and sectors. The ETFs shown in this exhibit are meant only to represent asset classes and not suggested investments. You should either do your own research or work with a financial advisor in making investments choices

U.S. Equity Investments	
Total Stock Market Index	**Symbol**
Vanguard Total U.S. Market ETF	VTI
iShares Core S&P Total U.S. Stock Market ETF	ITOT
Large Cap Stock Market Index	**Symbol**
iShares Core S&P 500 ETF	IVV
Dimensional Funds US Large Cap Equity Portfolio	DUSQX
iShares Morningstar Large-Cap Growth ETF	JKE
iShares Morningstar Large-Cap Value ETF	JKF
Mid Cap Stock Market Index	**Symbol**
Vanguard Mid-Cap ETF	VO
iShares S&P Mid-Cap 400 Growth ETF	IJK
iShares S&P Mid-Cap 400 Value ETF	IJJ
Small Cap Stock Market Index	**Symbol**
Vanguard Small-Cap ETF	VB
iShares S&P Small-Cap 600 Growth ETF	IJT
iShares S&P Small-Cap 600 Value ETF	IJS
Micro Cap Stocks	**Symbol**
iShares Micro-cap ETF	IWC

(Left margin, vertical text: Increased Expected Return — Increased Expected Risk)

When examining this exhibit, be aware that there are numerous studies available that will advise you to overweight one sector or style of the U.S. equity market as opposed to others. For example, some of the better-known research by Nobel Prize winners Eugene Fama and Kenneth French suggests that there is both a size and value premium when investing in equities. Based on the findings of their study, one would conclude that equity investors should favor small cap and value stocks to realize return premiums compared to the rest of the stock market. We will let you review such studies yourself to decide which U.S. equity investments best fit your portfolio.

International Equities

International markets can provide you with the opportunity to diversify your investments. This diversification comes with additional risk in the form of (i) foreign currency fluctuations (ii) political risk (iii) trading risk (iv) regulatory risk and (v) information risk. You can invest in international equities through developed, emerging or frontier foreign markets. The categorization of foreign markets is based on such information as size of Gross Domestic Product (GDP), government regulations and the development of capital markets. Typically, the less advanced a foreign market, the greater the volatility, but the greater the potential for returns.

Developed - there is no one set definition of a developed economy, but it most often refers to a country with a relatively high level of economic growth and security. Some of the most common criteria for evaluating a country's degree of development are per capita income or gross domestic product (GDP), level of industrialization, general standard of living and the amount of widespread infrastructure. Countries include among others Japan, Hong Kong and the countries of the European Union.

Emerging - nations that are becoming more advanced, demonstrated by some liquidity in local debt and equity markets as well as the existence of market exchange/regulatory bodies. Emerging markets generally do not have the level of market efficiency and strict standards in accounting and securities regulation to be on par with advanced economies. Countries include among others China, South Korea, India, South Africa, Brazil and Mexico.

Frontier - less advanced capital markets from the emerging world are sometimes referred to as "pre-emerging" or "frontier". Some of the risks you face in these frontier markets are political instability, poor liquidity, inadequate regulation, sub-standard financial reporting and large currency fluctuations. In addition, many markets are overly dependent on commodities, which can be quite volatile. Countries include among others Argentina, Vietnam, Kenya, Kuwait and Nigeria.

There are a number of indexes that allow you low-cost, liquid access to foreign markets. As the universe of ETFs has expanded you can invest in more and more distinct categories of the foreign equity market.

The ETFs shown are meant only to represent foreign equity asset classes and not as suggested investments. You should either do your own research or work with a financial advisor in making investment selections. You should thoroughly analyze your investment portfolio and the impact of foreign equities on it. Keep in mind that historically, foreign equities have provided diversification benefits, but correlations between foreign and U.S. equities have risen over time.

Increased Expected Return ↓ **Increased Expected Risk**

Foreign Equity Investments	
Developed International Equities	**Symbol**
iShares Core MSCI EAFE ETF	IEFA
DFA International Core Equity Portfolio	DFIEX
Vanguard International Value	VTRIX
Vanguard International Growth	VWIGX
Emerging Market Equities	**Symbol**
Vanguard Emerging Markets	VEIEX
iShares Core MSCI Emerging Markets ETF	IEMG
Frontier Market Equities	**Symbol**
iShares MSCI Frontier 100 ETF	FM

Quick Tip: *you can find further detail on Fama and French on the Dimensional Fund Advisor website http://us.dimensional.com/.*

What are the characteristics of the fixed income asset class?

Fixed income (bond) investors lend money to a company or other entity that is obligated to make regular interest payments to the investor plus pay back the initial borrowed principal on time. The rate of interest an issuer will pay on its bonds is dependent on the issuers financial health and the security supporting the bond (can assets be sold to make bond payments if need be?). Fixed income holdings are used to lower portfolio volatility and are subject to different risks than equities including:

Interest rate risk – the risk that arises for bond owners from fluctuating interest rates. The level of risk depends on two things, the bond's time to maturity, and the coupon rate of the bond. As interest rates increase, the opportunity cost of holding your current bond increases since you could realize greater yields by switching to another similar, but higher interest rate bond.

Maturity risk – maturities can be short-term (3 years or less), medium-term (4 – 9 years) or long-term (10 or more years). The longer a bond's term until maturity, the greater the bond's risk (more time to maturity provides greater opportunity to default).

Reinvestment risk – is the risk that future coupons from a bond will not be reinvested at the prevailing interest rate when the bond was initially purchased. Reinvestment risk is most applicable when interest rates are declining.

Credit/Default risk – the risk of loss stemming from a borrower's failure to repay a loan or otherwise meet a contractual obligation. Credit risk is measured by a number of credit rating agencies including Moodys and Standard & Poors.

There are several fixed income categories with unique risk and return characteristics. Although the categorization of fixed income is almost endless, a few of the broader, more investable fixed income categories are described here.

Government bonds – these are debt obligations of the U.S. government and can be offered as bills, notes and bonds. When you buy a U.S. Treasury security, you are lending money to the federal government for a specified period of time. Because these debt obligations are backed by the "full faith and credit" of the government, U.S. Treasury securities are generally considered the safest of all investments. This unique degree of safety results in interest rates (returns) that are lower than riskier debt securities.

Investment grade bonds – a bond whose credit quality is considered to be among the highest by independent bond-rating agencies. Due to the high credit quality, investors can expect lower returns from these bonds than the returns from high yield (junk) bonds.

High yield bonds – known as "junk bonds" these are bonds with a credit rating of BB or lower. These bonds are subject to greater price volatility and credit risk than other types of bonds. There are greater returns available to those willing to take on the additional risk of these lower-quality bonds.

Mortgage-backed bonds – a type of asset-backed security secured by a mortgage or collection of mortgages. The mortgages are sold to a group of individuals (can be a government agency or investment bank) that securitizes loans together into an instrument that investors can buy. The mortgages of an MBS may be residential or commercial.

Tax-free Municipals – tax-exempt bonds issued by state, city, and/or local governments. The interest payments for this type of bond are not subject to federal taxation and in some cases are not subject to state or local taxes.

Foreign debt – can be developed or emerging market debt. You must be careful when investing in foreign bonds as they can be more expensive and less liquid in many situations then their domestic counterparts. This debt can be issued in multiple forms and currencies.

Treasury Inflation Protected Securities (TIPS) – are Treasury securities issued by the U.S. government that have many of the characteristics of Treasuries, but that protect against inflation as measured by the Consumer Price Index (CPI).

The presence of fixed income in your portfolio can be an extremely useful way to generate steady streams of income to meet cash flow and liability needs. In addition to making fixed income investments through individual bonds and loans, you are increasingly able to access different parts of the fixed income market through low-cost Exchange Traded Funds (ETFs).

Fixed Income Investments	
Total Bond Market Funds	**Symbol**
Vanguard Total Bond Market	VBMFX
iShares Barclays Aggregate	AGG
Treasury Inflation-Protected Bonds	**Symbol**
Vanguard Inflation-Protected Securities	VIPSX
iShares Barclays TIPS Bond	TIP
Municipal Bonds	**Symbol**
Vanguard Interim Tax-exempt	VWITX
Vanguard Limited Term Tax-exempt	VMLTX
High-yield Bonds	**Symbol**
Vanguard High-Yield Corporate Bonds	VIPSX
Foreign Bonds	**Symbol**
iShares S&P/Citigroup International Treasury Bond	IGOV
iShares JP Morgan USD Emerging Markets	EMB

Increased Expected Return / *Increased Expected Risk*

Quick Tip: *the measurements of bond credit quality can be found here.*
https://www.fidelity.com/learning-center/investment-products/fixed-income-bonds/bond-ratings.

What are the characteristics of the alternative investment asset classes?

Alternative investments such as real estate, hedge funds, private equity and commodities have become much more mainstream and many popular endowment managers have often pointed to this style of investment as a reason for periods of outsized returns. These types of investments can be difficult to invest in though due to their high cost, illiquidity and lack of transparency. The outsized returns these alternative investments can at times provide don't come without risk or potential drawbacks. When considering an allocation to alternative investments, be sure to perform extensive research and make sure your portfolio can handle these types of investments.

Real estate - a separate asset class from stocks and bonds that has at times provided diversification from the other major asset classes. Although a steep housing correction between 2007 and 2009 injected fear in investors, real estate, particularly in the form of Real Estate Investment Trusts (REITs) has become increasingly popular. Outside of owning your own home, investments in real estate can be accomplished either directly or through an investment vehicle such as the previously mentioned REITs. A direct investment in real estate provides more control, but also additional headaches if you are responsible for things such as maintenance and collection of rents. REITs are designed as a tax efficient vehicle through which you can own a diversified real estate portfolio. As long as they comply with certain IRS requirements, REITs are structured so that in most cases they are exempt from federal and state income taxes. The risk and return characteristics of REITs have become much more similar to the equity markets over time, but real estate still remains a quality option to improve risk adjusted returns in a diversified portfolio.

Commodities – generally categorized as food (sugar, corn, oats), basic materials (steel, aluminum), metals (silver, gold) and energy-related items (crude oil, natural gas, electricity). The supply and demand dynamics of commodities can be out of balance for long periods leading to the "boom / bust" nature of commodities. Advocates of commodities believe they are a quality inflation hedge. In reality though, commodities have been much more volatile than inflation, offsetting their potential as a hedge. In addition, commodities never truly generate earnings the way a corporation does. When investing in commodities, particularly commodity funds, you need to be aware of the fee and tax issues that can arise from the high turnover of the underlying assets in these funds.

Hedge funds and private equity funds – hedge funds can pursue a large number of strategies including long-short, event-driven, distressed investing and merger arbitrage among others. Be sure to familiarize yourself with the type of strategy prior to investing. Private equity funds generally take the form of a direct investment into an underlying company. The type of company and form of investment can vary. Many times hedge funds and private equity funds can be exclusive, meaning a very high minimum investment is required just to get access to the fund. Although improvements have been made with regards to investor clarity, hedge funds and private equity funds can still lack transparency. Some funds require a lock-up, meaning you are unable to withdraw your investment until a certain period of time has elapsed. Fees for hedge funds and private equity funds can be quite high and historical performance numbers for the industry tend to be positively skewed as failed funds are not included in performance statistics.

When you are looking to diversify your portfolio, simply adding alternative asset classes without any analysis or insight into the risk of the asset class may not have the desired effect. You should be able to get almost, if not all of the diversification and performance you need from your portfolio through the use of traditional asset classes. In addition, the Alternative investment ETFs and indexes are not quite as straight-forward as the indexes that track other asset classes.

Alternative Investments	
Real Estate Investment Trusts	**Symbol**
Vanguard REIT ETF	VNQ
iShares U.S. Real estate ETF	IYR
Commodities	**Symbol**
iPath Bloomberg Commodity ETN	DJP
iPath S&P GSCI Total Return ETN	GSP

How should I forecast future asset class risk and returns?

Matching current assets and income streams with future liabilities is challenging. Your return expectations must be reasonable, and your projections must be prudent. A part of your Financial Plan and asset allocation strategy will be the formulation of realistic expectations for the assets you will use in your investment portfolio. There is a strong relationship between an asset classes' market risks and the asset classes' longer-term returns. Forecasting always involves some type of analysis of historical risk and return. Markets are much too volatile to be predicted with accuracy in the short-term, but an asset classes' historical risk and return statistics will be useful in constructing a portfolio to help meet your long-term needs. Your projections will never match actual outcomes exactly, and results may end up below your expectations. This means you can't construct your Financial Plan as if your projections will be met precisely. You should make sure the success of your Financial Plan is still possible in multiple scenarios.

Despite disagreements among the experts that construct them, most long-term asset class forecasts fall within a reasonable range. These forecasts can be a useful guide as you construct a Financial Plan. I won't provide you with projections, but investment firms such as Morgan Stanley and Ibbotson annually provide data on asset class returns and risk from which many other reputable firms derive their projections. A summary of these projections are shown here.

Asset Class Returns	
Emerging Market Stocks	9.8%
Small Cap Stocks	8.5%
Large Cap Stocks	6.7%
Developed Foreign Stocks	5.7%
Fixed Income	4.6%
Cash	1.3%

Asset class returns from 2002 - 2016. Source: Bloomberg, FactSet, MSCI, Russell, Standard & Poor's, JP Morgan Asset Management.

A well-diversified portfolio may hold a combination of several asset classes, categories, styles and sectors. When estimating long-term asset class expectations, you should have some knowledge of how asset classes move together (if one asset class rises in price does the price of the other asset class fall?). This relationship in asset class movement is called correlation. Asset classes that move in the same direction at the same time have positive correlation, while asset classes that move in different directions at the same time have negative correlations. Negative correlation is desirable in a portfolio because as the value of one set of assets declines, these losses will be offset by gains in the other asset class, reducing overall portfolio volatility. Negative correlation between two asset classes is extremely rare though and correlations tend to rise during bear (down) markets when investors most need diversification. It is difficult to predict future asset class correlations and realistically, most investment portfolios can at best hope to have a low positive correlation. In this asset class correlation matrix, as the correlation between two asset classes approaches 1.0, the movement of one asset class will more closely mimic the other and vice versa.

Asset Class Correlations and Volatility											
	US Lg Cap	EAFE	EME	Bonds	Corp HY	Munis	Currencies	EMD	Cmdts.	REITs	Hedge Funds	Private Equity
US Lg Cap	1.00	0.89	0.79	0.29	0.75	0.10	0.45	0.62	0.53	0.79	0.82	0.84
EAFE		1.00	0.91	0.13	0.80	0.02	0.64	0.73	0.60	0.68	0.86	0.82
EME			1.00	0.01	0.88	0.12	0.68	0.85	0.67	0.59	0.86	0.78
Bonds				1.00	0.06	0.80	0.23	0.26	0.11	0.00	0.19	0.25
Corp HY					1.00	0.11	0.51	0.88	0.66	0.67	0.82	0.72
Munis						1.00	0.22	0.45	0.09	0.07	0.01	0.13
Currencies							1.00	0.62	0.62	0.40	0.47	0.55
EMD								1.00	0.59	0.60	0.71	0.62
Cmdts.									1.00	0.40	0.72	0.71
REITs										1.00	0.56	0.66
Hedge Funds											1.00	0.86
Private Equity												1.00

Note: Numbers in red represent negative correlations. Source: JP morgan Q3 2017 Guide to the Markets.

What is the capital gains tax on investments?

Almost everything you own and use for personal or investment purposes is a capital asset. Some of the most common capital assets are stocks and bonds held for investment. Gains and losses you experience on these capital assets are treated a bit differently than your income for tax purposes. When you sell a capital asset, the difference between your adjusted basis, which is generally the assets cost to you, and the sale proceeds is either a capital gain or capital loss. Capital losses can be used to offset capital gains. In addition, capital losses in excess of capital gains can be used to offset your taxable income by up to $3,000 annually. Unfortunately, you are not able to use losses from the sale of personal-use assets such as your home or car to offset your taxable income.

Capital gains and losses are classified as either short-term or long-term for the purposes of calculating your capital gains tax. If you hold an asset for more than one year it will be considered long-term. If your holding period for an asset is less than one year it is considered short-term. If you realize a capital gain upon the sale of an asset with a short-term holding period, the realized gain will be taxed at the same rate as your ordinary income. This rate will more than likely be greater than the capital gains tax rate you pay if the asset holding period is long-term. If you sell an asset after a long-term holding period for a gain, this gain will be taxed at a rate that is more advantageous than the tax rate applied to your ordinary income. This more advantageous rate is known as the capital gains tax rate.

- If you are in the 10% or 15% federal ordinary income tax bracket, you will not be taxed on long-term capital gains.
- For all ordinary income tax brackets above 15%, but below the top bracket of 39.6%, you will pay 15% on long-term capital gains.
- For those whose taxable income is higher than the maximum income tax bracket of 39.6%, the tax rate on long-term capital gains is 20%.

As a result of the Tax Cuts and Jobs Act of 2017 the tax brackets above will be changed to specific taxable income levels starting in 2018.

Tax rate	Joint Return	Individual
0%	not over $77,200	not over $38,600
15%	not over $479,000	not over $425,800
20%	over $479,000	over $425,800

When it comes to your portfolio, a short-term holding period is less advantageous for you tax-wise than a long-term holding period and the moral of the story is to avoid short-term gains where possible. For more detail on the taxation of different asset classes and how you can take advantage of "tax location" strategies, please refer to Appendix A of this book.

Starting in 2013, you could owe a 3.8% Medicare tax on some of or all your net investment income. This Medicare tax will apply to either the amount of your Modified Adjusted Gross Income (MAGI) that exceeds certain thresholds, or apply directly to your investment income, whichever is less. Check the IRS website for details.

Further Resources

- **www.iShares.com** – this is BlackRock's ETF-centric website. You can learn a great deal about ETFs and use the helpful portfolio management tools on the site. The website provides specific help for your retirement goals at "iRetire".

- **www.morningstar.com** – although this is a subscription-based website, there is plenty of free information on financial planning, investments and the capital markets. Good day-to-day articles on the markets provided.

- **www.etf.com** – website dedicated to ETFs, that provides all sorts of information regarding trends, fund flows, strategies and the quality of any ETF you want to look up. You will be required to sign-up for certain sections of the website.

- **www.us.dimensional.com** – dedicated website that offers ETFs and products based on an application of the studies and findings of Eugene Fama and Kenneth French. Website has good academic and qualitative information on passive investment management.

Books:

Darst, David M. *The Art of Asset Allocation*. The McGraw Hill Companies. 2008. Provides an introduction and overview of asset allocation including its importance, ramifications of not implementing asset allocation and how asset allocation should fit into your financial planning. Great source, but be sure to look for updates to information.

Gibson, Roger C. *Asset Allocation: Balancing Financial Risk.* **The McGraw Hill Companies. 2013.**

Provides step-by-step guidelines for designing and implementing portfolio allocation strategies. Shows how active management has failed to beat markets over time and educates the reader on capital markets, investor behavior and portfolio management principles.

PART II: FINANCIAL PLANNING TOPICS

Chapter 3: Saving for Education

✓ Estimate the amount you will need to fund your children's higher education needs then figure out the annual savings required to meet this goal.

✓ Learn about the types of savings vehicles (529 Accounts, Coverdell, tax credits) that can help you reach your higher education goals.

✓ Master the financial aid process, particularly the FAFSA Form.

College tuition will be one of, if not the largest expense you will pay for in your lifetime. College costs will be compounded by the number of children you will support as they pursue their higher education goals. Although many view education as an expense, this use of your resources more closely resembles an investment. A college diploma will serve as the variable that allows your child to earn much more over the course of their lifetime as compared to a peer that only receives a high school degree.

The how and when of financing higher education must be thoroughly analyzed. Many strategies and investment vehicles are available to help you execute an education savings plan. The factors you will need to look at when examining methods of saving include:

- Future investment growth
- Tax implications
- Investment risk
- Account ownership (including beneficiaries)
- Fees and expenses

What will College Cost Me?

Below is an estimate of the annual costs to attend a public or private university. In addition to the high ticket price of attending college, investors must battle elevated levels of inflation. According to the College Board, the price of college has risen at 3.5% above the average rate of inflation over the past few decades.

	Public Two-Year	Public Four-Year (in-State)	Public Four-Year (out-of-State)	Private Four-Year
Education Expenses				
Tuition and Fees				
2016-2017	$3,520	$9,650	$24,930	$33,480
2015-2016	$3,440	$9,420	$24,070	$32,330
$ Change	$80	$230	$860	$1,150
% Change	2.3%	2.4%	3.6%	3.6%
Room and Board				
2016-2017	$8,060	$10,440	$10,440	$11,890
2015-2016	$7,930	$10,150	$10,150	$11,540
$ Change	$130	$290	$290	$350
% Change	1.6%	2.9%	2.9%	3.0%
Tuition and Fees + Room and Board				
2016-2017	$11,580	$20,090	$35,370	$45,370
2015-2016	$11,370	$19,570	$34,220	$43,870
$ Change	$210	$520	$1,150	$1,500
% Change	1.8%	2.7%	3.4%	3.4%

Source: The College Board, Annual Survey of Colleges. Completed October 2016.

Prices in Table are not adjusted for inflation. Prices reported for 2015-16 have been revised and may differ from those reported in Trends in College Pricing 2015. Public two-year room and board charges are based on commuter housing and food costs. Tuition and fee figures for the for-profit sector should be interpreted with caution because of the low response rate.

There are far too many variables for a "one size fits all" education plan, but estimating your needed monthly education savings as part of creating a personal cash flow budget is a good exercise. Required annual savings vary depending on when in your child's life you begin setting aside funds. Rising tuition costs are tough news for those of us who will be covering these expenses in the future, but the good news is that there are a number of tax-advantaged ways to save for higher education.

Quick Tip: *there are a number of free quality college cost estimators including those provided by savingforcollege.com, the College Board and Vanguard.*

How do I apply for financial aid?

To apply for federal student aid, you need to complete the Free Application for Federal Student Aid more commonly known as FAFSA. Many states and colleges use your FAFSA data to determine your eligibility for state and school specific aid. If you are not ready or do not need to file the actual FAFSA form you can fill out a "FAFSA4caster" on the student.ed.gov website. The "FAFSA4caster" will provide you with important estimated figures such as your Federal Pell Grant (if applicable), Federal Work Study, subsidized and unsubsidized loan amounts as well as your Expected Family Contribution.

For any school year you want to apply for federal aid, you will need to file your FAFSA application between January 1st and June 30th, but the earlier you submit the application the better. In addition, be sure to check for school and state specific deadlines when applying for student aid.

The documents you will need to complete the FAFSA form include your:
- Social Security card
- Driver's license or permanent resident card
- W-2 forms for most recent year and any other records of money earned
- Most recent income tax return
- Current investment records and bank statements
- Current business and farm records
- Records of Federal Work-Study and any student grants, scholarships or federal aid

After receiving your completed application, a FAFSA processor will analyze your data and calculate your Expected Family Contribution. Your Expected Family Contribution is an estimate of your and/or your student's ability to contribute to post-secondary education expenses. Within 2 – 3 days you will receive a Student

Aid Report (SAR) verifying the information you provided in your FAFSA form. You should receive your results from FAFSA within 7 – 10 days. You can check the status of your application by calling 1-800-4FEDAID.

Your FAFSA results will be sent to the schools that you list on your FAFSA application. The schools you listed will then notify you of your financial aid package. Although it is usually not the case, schools can wait until just before classes begin to inform you of the aid you have qualified for.

Be sure to contact your state department of education regarding grants or other state-related student aid. You can find the contact information for your state department of education at www2.ed.gov. In addition, get in touch with the financial aid office of the school you may attend to see if there are any school-specific forms related to student aid you need to fill out.

Quick Tip: you can begin the financial aid process and access the FAFSA form by setting up a profile at studentaid.ed.gov.

What determines the amount of financial aid a student receives?

In addition to the student's merit, need-based sources of aid will depend on (i) the cost of the school the student will attend (calculation is based on Federal guidelines) and (ii) the value of outside resources, such as scholarships or a direct payment on the student's behalf to the institution. These sources will reduce the student's need-based aid.

The key figure in determining your financial aid package is your Expected Family Contribution. This is the amount you will be expected to pay for college based on your financial circumstances. This figure is determined annually using the data you provide in your FAFSA form. The Expected Family Contribution considers the income and assets of both student and parent. The expected contribution is then divided by the number of family members in college at least part-time. The Expected Family Contribution formula counts the financial resources below as available to pay for college:

- 20% of student's assets
- 50% of student's income
- 2.6% - 5.6% of parent's assets (cash, investments and business interests)
- 22% - 47% of parent's income (based on a sliding income scale)

Given the percentages applied to your income and assets, some of the more favorable assets to own when it comes time to apply for student financial aid include:

- Individual Retirement Accounts (IRAs) and 401(k) accounts are not counted at all when calculating the Expected Family Contribution. There is no penalty on withdrawals from these types of accounts when the proceeds are used to pay for higher education, but you will pay taxes on the withdrawal and the entire withdrawal will count as parental income on the following years FAFSA application.

- Equity in a primary home, your stake in a family-owned business, insurance policies and annuities are all excluded when it comes to determining your Expected Family Contribution.

- If a parent or student owns a 529 college savings account or a Coverdell Education Savings Account, up to 5.6% of the value is included when calculating the Expected Family Contribution. If a grandparent owns one of these accounts, none of the value counts towards the Expected Family Contribution. Funds used from a grandparent owned 529 count as student income the following year, so it is best practice to try and use a grandparent 529 at a point when it will not increase student income (typically the student's final year of school).

What tax incentives are available to help me save for education?

Be sure to coordinate the various tax credits and deductions summarized below and take note of the forms needed to claim these credits and deductions.

- The **American Opportunity Tax Credit** is a tax credit (a direct offset to taxable income) for 100% of the first $2,000 of qualified post-secondary education expenses paid in a tax year, plus 25% of the next $2,000 of qualified expenses. The maximum allowed credit is $2,500 per student. The qualified education expenses include tuition, enrollment fees, and other related expenses (room and board is not considered a qualified expense) for the taxpayer, spouse or dependent. The student must be enrolled no less than part-time and there is a limit of four years in which this credit can be claimed for one student. A portion (40%) of the American Opportunity Tax Credit is refundable, so even if you owe no taxes, you can receive cash as a result of the tax credit. The American Opportunity Tax Credit is subject to a phase out based on the taxpayer's Modified Adjusted Gross Income (MAGI) (i) Married Filing Jointly: $160,000 - $180,000 and (ii) All other filers: $80,000 - $90,000.

- The **Lifetime Learning Credit** provides an annual per taxpayer reimbursement for qualified tuition and related expenses per family in the amount of $2,000 per year. A 20% factor applies to a maximum of $10,000 of qualified expenses. The Lifetime Learning Credit is available for undergraduate, graduate or professional degree programs and part-time enrollment is not required (a bit less restrictive than the American Opportunity Tax Credit). A Lifetime Learning Credit can be claimed for an unlimited number of years. The Lifetime Learning Credit is subject to phase out based on the taxpayers Modified Adjusted Gross Income (MAGI) (i) Married Filing Jointly: $111,000 - $131,000 and (ii) All other filers: $55,000 - $65,000. The American Opportunity Tax Credit and the Lifetime Learning Credit can't be claimed in the same year by the same student.

- Under the **Employer's Educational Assistance Program**, an employer can reimburse an employee's tuition (graduate and undergraduate) and the benefits are excluded from the employee's income up to $5,250 per year. You are unable to claim any education tax credits on the same expenses used for Employer's Educational Assistance Program.

- Interest paid on loans incurred solely to pay qualified higher education expenses can be deducted up to a maximum amount of $2,500 annually. These deductions are subject to limitation based on the taxpayers Modified Adjusted Gross Income (MAGI) (i) Married Filing Jointly: $160,000 and (ii) All other filers: $80,000.

Quick Tip: for the American Opportunity and Lifetime Learning Credit you will receive a Form 1098-T from the educational institution to help you calculate your Tax Credit. You will then claim your tax credit by completing Form 8863 (available directly on the IRS website) and attaching it to your Form 1040.

What are the most advantageous accounts to help save for education?

There are a handful of savings vehicles you can use as part of an education savings plan. Each type of account we describe has different characteristics and benefits. Any one or a combination of more than one of these accounts may fit your needs.

- A **529 Investment Program** (a 529) is a mainstay in any college savings plan. A 529 is an educational savings program operated by a state or educational institution named after Section 529 of the Internal Revenue Code. A 529 allows you to open an account and make contributions for any individual beneficiary you choose (child, grandchild, neighbor or even yourself). All 529s are state-sponsored and most are open to residents of any state. In addition, it generally doesn't matter where the beneficiary attends college. The contributions you make to a 529 are after-tax (income tax has already been deducted), but investments in a 529 grow tax-deferred and can be withdrawn free of tax if they are used for qualified higher education expenses. These qualified expenses include tuition, fees, books, supplies and room and board. The minimum initial investment requirements for 529s are quite low.
  - Unlike many other investment accounts, 529s have no income, or age limits. There are typically lifetime contribution limits, but these are extremely high and you should check with the 529 you enroll in.
  - Your state may offer a state income tax deduction for the contributions you make to a 529 Investment Program. For example, a married couple filing jointly can receive a $10,000 state tax deduction for contributing to a New York State 529 College Savings Program.
  - 529s are extremely flexible and you may change the beneficiary of the account to another qualifying family member or roll your existing 529 into a

different state's 529 Investment Program without triggering any taxes if no other rollover has occurred in the previous 12 months. You can change investments in your 529 Investment program two times per year or upon the change of a beneficiary.

- As a result of the Tax Cuts and Jobs Act of 2017, 529s can now be used to pay for educational expenses at private institutions for kindergarten through Grade 12.

- The value of your 529 is not included in your gross estate for estate planning purposes. If you contribute to a 529 it will be treated as a gift (gift taxes are not applicable until death). If your contribution is greater than the annual gifting limits it will be subject to gift taxes. When it comes to gift taxes you can take advantage of a special five-year election that allows you to put roughly $70,000 into a 529 without any gift tax implications. This election uses your annual gifting exclusions for the next 5 years. You can find out more about gifting and estate planning later in this book.

- With a 529, the beneficiary has no legal rights of ownership. You own the account and invest as you see fit on the beneficiary's behalf.

- For each 529 you own, you will receive periodic investment statements, but no tax documents until you begin withdrawing funds from your 529. Once withdrawals begin there is no tax if your withdrawals do not exceed qualified higher education expenses (in which case there is a 10% penalty tax). When you start making withdrawals you will receive a Form 1099-Q detailing your 529 withdrawals. Be sure to save your 1099-Q Forms as well as documentation that your 529 withdrawals were spent on qualified expenses.

- Signing up for a 529 is easy and inexpensive. In addition to the underlying mutual fund fees, 529 plans are professionally managed so a modest investment fee will be charged. A 529 program is not meant to be expensive, so be careful if you sign up for a 529 through a financial advisor. Be sure to find out any extra fees they will charge you.

- A 529 can be prepaid. Under this type of program, you can make an immediate payment or a series of payments and the 529 promises to pay future tuition and fees at a specified college or university. Though a pre-paid 529 is not as flexible as a "normal" 529, it can help hedge tuition inflation. A pre-paid program can often be converted to benefits at non-specified universities.

- A **Coverdell Education Savings Account** ("Coverdell") lets parents, grandparents, other family members or even your child contribute money to a tax-advantaged account for future education expenses. These types of accounts are offered through several financial institutions such as Schwab, TD Ameritrade etc. Contributions to a Coverdell are not tax deductible, but like a 529, earnings in a Coverdell are tax-deferred and can be withdrawn free of tax in the year the beneficiary incurs qualified education expenses. When you open a Coverdell you will sign an agreement that names a beneficiary and a "responsible individual" which is usually required to be a parent. The agreement will indicate if the beneficiary will assume control of the account at 18 or if control of the account remains with you.
  - The beneficiary of a Coverdell ESA must be under 18 at the time the account is opened. The combined contributions on behalf of any one child may not exceed an annual contribution limit of $2,000. Any excess contributions will be assessed an excise tax. You have until April 15th of the following year to fund a Coverdell ESA.
  - A contributor to a Coverdell must have income less than $190,000 if married filing jointly or $95,000 for all other filers to make the maximum $2,000 annual contribution. Partial contributions are allowed for incomes up to $220,000 if married filing jointly or $110,000 for all other filers.

- A Coverdell ESA can include a wider range of investments as compared to a 529 Investment Program where the investment offerings are more limited. You can change your investments in your Coverdell ESA as often as you'd like and roll funds into another Coverdell ESA once every 12 months.

- Unlike 529 Investment Programs which may only be used for higher education expenses, funds can be withdrawn from a Coverdell tax-free to pay elementary and secondary school costs. Qualifying expenses can include things like transportation, uniforms, or even internet access.

- Funds must be distributed from a Coverdell by age 30 (unless the beneficiary has special needs). At age 30, the account terminates and the remaining assets are subject to a 10% penalty on all earnings. You can transfer a Coverdell to another qualifying family member under the age of 30.

- In most states, minors are unable to directly own stocks, bonds, mutual funds, annuities and life insurance policies. Therefore, you are not able to simply transfer assets to your minor child (potentially lowering your tax bill) and must transfer the assets to a trust instead. The **Uniform Gift to Minors Act (UGMA)** was established as a simple way to accomplish this. The **Uniform Transfer to Minors Act (UTMA)** is like a UGMA, but allows minors to own other types of property and for transfers to occur through inheritance. To establish the account, the donor appoints a custodian (trustee) and irrevocably gifts money to the trust. Contributing money to a UGMA account on another person's behalf could be subject to gift tax; however, the Internal Revenue Code of the United States allows you to give up to the annual gift tax exclusion ($15,000 for and individual and $30,000 for couples in 2018) to another person without any gift tax consequences. The money then belongs to the minor, but can't be accessed until they reach the age of trust termination. The age of termination varies by state, but is typically between the ages of 18 and 21.

- Any money in a UGMA and UTMA for which you are the custodian and the child has not yet reached the age of termination will be counted as part of your taxable estate.

- The income from a UGMA or UTMA must be reported on the child's tax return and is subject to Kiddie Tax Rules. The IRS provides detailed instructions on the calculation of your child's tax on Form 8615. Parents are responsible for filing an income tax return on behalf of the child. Children older than 14 must sign their own tax returns. The Kiddie Tax applies to your child's unearned income. In 2018, the first $1,050 of your child's unearned income is not taxed, the next $1,050 of unearned income is taxed at your child's lower rate and any unearned income above $2,100 is taxed at your maximum rate.

- Neither the donor nor the custodian can place any restrictions on the minor's use of money once they reach the age of trust termination. So, it is possible the funds will not be used to fund education expenses.

- When funding a UGMA or UTMA you should analyze the benefit of having the first $2,100 of unearned income taxed at a lower rate against the less favorable impact these accounts may have on your Expected Family Contribution because they are considered your child's assets.

- After 1989, if they are purchased by someone over 24 years old, a Series EE or Series I Savings Bond can be redeemed and the interest earned on these bonds will be tax-free if the proceeds are used for higher education expenses. Qualified higher education expenses include rolling over the funds from the Series EE or Series I Savings Bond into a qualified tuition program such as a 529 Investment Program or a Coverdell ESA.
  - The redemption benefit for Series I and Series EE is subject to a phase-out in the years in which the bonds are redeemed. The benefit phases out if your Modified Adjusted Gross Income (MAGI) is $116,300.

- $146,300 for joint returns and $77,550 - $92,550 for other returns. Married taxpayers filing separately do not qualify.

Quick Tips: be sure to check out your own states 529 plan offering at www.collegesavings.org. When thinking about your 529 tax deduction, if you are subject to the top 2017 New York State tax bracket of 8.82%, you could save $882 on a $10,000 investment. You can easily open a UGMA or UTMA account numerous places including Fidelity and Vanguard.

What government aid is available to help fund education costs?

Higher education expenses you are unable to fund through scholarships, aid from the institution or your own assets can be covered by government grants and loans. By filling out your FAFSA application you will be eligible for this aid. The terms of these grants and loans vary and you should thoroughly review and understand all characteristics of the applicable grant or loan prior to accepting, especially because some carry elevated rates of interest.

- A **Federal Pell Grant** is an outright gift from the government based on the student's need and the cost of attending a chosen school. Only undergraduate students who have not previously received a bachelor's degree are eligible for these grants. The Federal Pell Grant Program is the largest need-based student aid program and the maximum amount of award changes each year depending on program funding. For 2018, the maximum Federal Pell Grant you can receive is $5,920.
- Students are automatically considered for the **Federal Supplemental Educational Opportunity Grant (SEOG)** program when they fill out their FAFSA application. You can receive between $100 and $4,000 annually and these funds generally do not need to be repaid. The program is managed by colleges instead of the federal government and the amounts awarded can vary.
- The **Federal Perkins Loan Program** is a federally funded program administered by colleges. The program provides loans of up to $5,500 per year for undergraduate students and $8,000 per year for graduate students. The cumulative limits are $27,500 for undergraduate loans and $60,000 for undergraduate and graduate loans combined.
  - Perkins loans have a 5.0% fixed interest rate, deferred repayment, a nine-month grace period and a maximum of 10 years to repay the loan.

Interest on a Perkins Loan is subsidized by the federal government while the student is in school and during the nine-month deferral period.

- Under the **Federal College Work-Study Program**, a student works 10 – 15 hours per week at a job that is typically on campus, to earn a portion of their financial aid package. The Federal College Work-Study Program is sponsored by the federal government, but administered by colleges and universities.

- **Subsidized Federal Stafford Loans** are based on financial need and the government pays the interest while the student is in school. Repayment is deferred until 6 months after student graduates. **Unsubsidized Federal Stafford Loans** are not based on financial need and the government does not pay the interest while the student is in school, but the interest may be capitalized. Maximum borrowings range from $3,500 to $12,500 annually depending on the student's education status (ex. Freshman vs. Senior), parent dependency status and if the loan is subsidized. Repayment options for the loan can take between 10 and 25 years and loan deferment and forbearance are available if you have trouble meeting your payment obligations. Interest rates on subsidized and unsubsidized loans for undergraduates are 4.45% and 6.0% for graduate or professional students in 2018. There is a fee for each loan disbursement of 1.066%.

- **Federal PLUS Loans** allow you to borrow up to the total cost of education less other financial aid awards. Loans are not made on the basis of financial need, but you must have a satisfactory credit history to borrow. Repayment of the loan must begin within 60 days of disbursement. The rate on these Federal PLUS loans is fixed at 7.0% for 2018 and there is an additional fee with each disbursement of 4.264%. Loans of graduate and independent students are placed into deferment while students are enrolled at least part-time and for an additional 6 months after that.

Quick Tip: a great source of further information on this topic is the Federal Student Aid website studentaid.ed.gov.

Should I save for retirement or save for college?

Ideally, saving for your dependent's higher education costs and saving for your own retirement will be part of the same financial plan and can fit in your cash flow budget. Even if you are only able to set aside very small amounts on a monthly basis for both of these goals you will be surprised at the amount that you are able to accumulate over time. Often times though, saving for both higher education costs and your retirement is just not possible. Although each individual's circumstances are different and there are no concrete rules, there are a number of reasons you should continue to fund your future retirement goals instead of putting away savings for college.

- Unlike higher education expenses, for which you are able to receive scholarships, grants and aid which can be paid back over time there is no way to supplement cash needs in retirement.

- Unlike funds you contribute to accounts earmarked for future education costs, many retirement savings plans such as a 401(k) and 403(b) you have through an employer will match the contributions you make to the retirement plan. In this case, contributions to your employer retirement plan should be maximized to take advantage of all employer matching.

- A retirement plan, such as a 401(k) or Individual Retirement Account (IRA) will not impact your chances of receiving financial aid for education as they do not count as assets in the calculation of your Expected Family Contribution.

- Although you will pay ordinary income tax, if you tap into an IRA to pay for higher education costs before the age of 59 ½ you will not pay the 10% penalty tax on these distributions that you otherwise would.

If you are a grandparent that already has enough money accumulated to ensure a comfortable retirement you may want to investigate using some of your resources to pay higher education expenses for a loved one.

- You can realize estate planning benefits through funds contributed to a 529. A 529 account is not considered part of your taxable estate even if you are the owner (you are not responsible for taxes once you pass away).
- Grandparents can actually help fund higher education expenses without incurring gift taxes by paying tuition costs directly to the institution (as opposed to making a payment to a parent or grandchild).
- Although the ownership of a 529 by a grandparent does not impact your student's financial aid eligibility, the use of funds in the account will count as student income in applying for aid the following year. Therefore, many grandparents wait until the final year of education to make payments from a 529 they own.

Further Resources

- **savingforcollege.com** – free website with great information on saving for college, the various accounts (529, Coverdell etc.) that can be used to save for higher education and how to receive government aid. You can access every state's 529 plan as well a very informative resource titled "Family Guide to College Savings" that is updated annually and available for download.

- **studentaid.ed.gov** – federal website with summary description of all types of available government financial aid. This is where you can access your FAFSA form as well as read up on exactly how to fill it out and applicable deadlines.

- **finaid.org** – free website with summaries of all different types of financial aid. Key differentiator with finaid.org is its extensive coverage of available scholarships and private sources of financial aid. Be sure to check out their Expected Family Contribution calculator.

- **Bigfuture.collegeboard.org** – provides an overview of all the different ways you can fund higher education costs. Useful calculators on the cost of college, Expected Family Contribution etc. as well as a more qualitative section on what the college "experience" may be like.

Books:

Joseph Hurley, CPA. *The Best Way to Save For College A Complete Guide to 529 Plans.* Savingforcollege.com. 2017.

Great guide for families and professionals written by the founder of the savingforcollege.com website. Directed towards financial advisors, but a good resource for anyone looking to learn about college savings strategies.

Getting Financial Aid 2018 Edition; The College Board

The all-important FAFSA form is explained with step-by-step instructions. The guide includes information and advice from experts on how to apply for aid, plus easy-to-compare college profiles giving the "financial aid picture" for more than 3,000 four-year and two-year colleges/technical schools.

Chapter 4: Understanding Insurance

✓ It is very difficult to obtain the insurance you may need by yourself. Understand the difference between an insurance agent and an insurance broker and find professionals you can trust.

✓ Review and understand the various forms of insurance available to you or that you may already have, including life insurance, homeowner's insurance, medical insurance, disability insurance, and automotive insurance.

✓ Learn the difference between the various types of life insurance, particularly term and permanent life insurance.

✓ Estimate the amount of life insurance and disability insurance you may need and understand the different estimate methodologies.

Generally, insurance doesn't enter the forefront of our minds until some life event forces it there. By design, insurance won't play much of a role in your everyday life, but it is extremely important for yourself and your loved ones that you have the correct insurance coverage as part of your Financial Plan.

The life, disability, home, medical and automotive insurance you have in place are just as important as any other part of your Financial Plan. Even if the other parts of your Financial Plan are strong, if a large gap in your insurance coverage is exposed, such an event can make it very difficult to reach your financial goals.

Although you may rely on others, such as an insurance agent or broker to help you with your insurance needs, it is important to have a solid understanding of your policy options yourself. In addition to the information we provide here, you may want to work with a trusted insurance professional to get up to speed on your policies and any additional insurance you may need. Always be cautious, and make sure insurance suggestions you receive are actually a good fit.

Quick Tip: *An insurance agent is an insurance company's representative and the agent's primary alliance is with the insurance company not the insurance buyer. An insurance broker represents the insured, and has no contractual requirements with an insurance carrier to sell their products.*

What are the unique legal characteristics of insurance contracts?

You can have numerous types of insurance, some of the more common types include life, disability, home, medical and automotive insurance policies. Regardless of the type of insurance, these contracts have a number of common characteristics that you should become familiar with. These characteristics include:

- First and foremost, an insurable interest. This is a relationship where the party that enters the insurance contract would incur a loss from the destruction, damage or death of the insured object.

- Insurance contracts abide by the indemnity principle which means your recovery will be to the extent of your financial loss. The exception to this is a life insurance policy where the recovery is the face value of the policy and not the value of the life insured.

- Insurance contracts are settled in one of three ways (i) actual cash value of the loss up to the value of the insurance contract (this method factors in depreciation) (ii) replacement cost (iii) stated value contracts set an agreed upon value to be covered by the insurer.

- Aside from life insurance contracts, insurance contracts are personally owned and can't be transferred or assigned to another person without the written consent of the insurance company.

- Insurance contracts are unilateral contracts meaning that only the insurer promises to perform, the policy owner does not actually promise to pay the premiums.

- If no loss occurs the insurer will pay nothing, alternatively if a loss occurs the insurer may pay the policy holder compensation that is greater than the actual premiums received.

What are some of the general provisions of life insurance contracts?

Life insurance is regulated at the state level, so although there is no "standard" life insurance contract, because all policies have to be approved by the applicable State Insurance Commissioner there tend to be a number of common provisions. These common life insurance provisions include:

- A life insurance policy is considered property. The owner may assign, transfer, and sometimes borrow against the policies value.
- The person to whom the proceeds are payable is called a beneficiary. Beneficiaries can be primary or contingent, revocable or irrevocable. A primary beneficiary is the first person or party entitled to the proceeds of the policy, while a contingent beneficiary or beneficiaries receive the proceeds if the primary beneficiary dies before the insured. A revocable beneficiary can be changed by the policy owner at any time, while an irrevocable beneficiary can't be changed by the policy owner.
- The incontestable clause states that a life insurance policy is incontestable once a certain period of time passes, usually 2 years.
- All life insurance policies have a grace period from the premium due date before the life insurance policy lapses. The policy owner typically has 30 or 31 days from the due date to pay the premium before the policy lapses.
- Life insurance contracts allow for a number of settlement options. Generally, death benefits are received tax free with proceeds in excess of principal treated as ordinary income for tax purposes. The receipt of benefits can be quite complex though, so be sure to consult with a tax professional or financial advisor regarding the tax implications of these different settlement options. Life insurance settlement options include:
  - Lump sum, where the death benefit is paid in full.

- The interest-only option is when the principal received from the policy remains invested with the insurance company while the interest earned on this principal is paid to the designated beneficiary.
- With fixed-period installments both principal and interest are paid over a specified period. With fixed-amount installments the proceeds are paid at a set dollar amount per month.
- A beneficiary can elect to be paid life insurance benefits as an annuity which is known as life income. The different types of annuities include:
  - In a single life annuity the beneficiary receives a specified amount of money periodically until the beneficiary dies at which time annuity payments cease.
  - A life annuity with period certain allows the beneficiary to be paid a specified amount periodically, for life, but the payments are guaranteed for a certain number of periods. In the event a beneficiary dies prior to the end of the specified period, payments continue to a contingent beneficiary.
  - A life annuity with refund allows the beneficiary to be paid a specified amount periodically. If the amount of payments received does not exceed the basis of the annuity when the beneficiary passes away, the remainder of the basis is paid to the contingent beneficiary.

How do I estimate the amount of life insurance I need?

As part of your life insurance decision, it is a useful exercise to estimate the value of your life insurance needs. Two of the more popular methods of this estimate are (i) the human life value method and (ii) the financial needs analysis method. You can use whichever methodology makes you most comfortable.

The human life value method projects your income through your remaining life expectancy including raises. A discount rate is then used to derive the present value of the life insurance policy you need. Cash flows can be adjusted downward for what you would have personally consumed or paid (ex. taxes on your income).

The financial needs analysis method examines all recurring expenses to dependent survivors and any unusual expenditures that result from the death of the policy holder. The financial needs incorporated in this analysis are outlined below. All of these needs should be adjusted for inflation where appropriate.

- A fund for final expenses including medical costs and funeral costs.
- A fund for "readjustment" during the period that occurs immediately following a policy holder's death when one-time costs are most likely to occur.
- The dependency period income fund is usually the period of highest needs because dependents require income for routine living (children, housing, pre-college expenses etc.).
- A mortgage payment fund is an effective way of reducing ongoing income needs by providing cash sufficient to pay off your existing mortgage. This same analysis you perform for your mortgage can be done to estimate what will be needed to pay future education expenses.

- Life income for a surviving spouse. This is income needed for a surviving spouse's retirement in addition to other sources of income such as Social Security.

The financial needs analysis method can be calculated in two ways, the first is the annuity approach which assumes that all life insurance proceeds will be consumed by the survivor (leaving no funds at the survivor's death). The second method is the purchasing power preservation model which provides surviving dependents with proceeds while maintaining the initial balance of the life insurance proceeds (for example, if the initial balance is $1 million, the remaining balance at death is $1 million).

Quick Tip: you can try to estimate needs yourself or use one of the many estimator tools offered by Insurance providers for example, TIAA has a "Lifewizard" tool https://www.tiaa.org/public/lifewizard.html.

What other factors should I consider when selecting a life insurance policy?

One of the most important insurance contracts you will ever own is your life insurance contract. Before you select a new life insurance contract or modify an existing life insurance contract, you should research some of the important elements of these contracts. You can take the following steps as part of this research.

- Examine the financial strength of the insurer. You can look at the analysis of insurance companies by various ratings agencies of the insurance company including A.M. Best, Fitch, Moody's and S&P. Other factors impacting the financial strength of insurers includes surplus reserves, investment portfolio quality, cash flows, liquidity, historical earnings stability and management team.

- Insurers can and will provide you with policy illustrations that are a hypothetical representation of how your policy will perform. The policy illustration will include:
  - Values guaranteed by the insurance company (ex. minimum earnings rate) as well as non-guaranteed values (ex. anticipated portfolio earnings). Be wary of a policy that has unreasonably high earnings expectations.
  - Mortality (policy holder death rates) assumptions are a large component of performance.
  - Interest rate assumptions are particularly important in whole life insurance policy projections where the insurer bears the investment risk.
  - Lapse experience (the number of holders that cease paying their premiums) is a key variable as policies with lower lapse rates tend to have lower pricing.
  - In addition to insurer financial strength and policy illustrations, you should obtain from the insurer their historical interest rate and dividend projections and compare these to actual historical results.

What are the different types of life insurance policies?

Once you have a good estimate of your life insurance requirements, you can look at the wide variety of policy options available to you. Most life insurance policies can be categorized as either term or permanent life insurance policies. Term life insurance policies provide you with coverage for a set period, usually between 10 and 30 years. Permanent life insurance policies provide coverage for the entirety of the policy owner's life. These policies combine a death benefit with a savings and/or investment feature. This makes permanent life insurance policies more expensive than comparable term life insurance alternatives. Common types of permanent life insurance include Whole, Variable and Universal life insurance policies.

Term life insurance - pure insurance protection that pays a death benefit if the insured dies during a specified timeframe. Your protection ceases at the end of a selected term (usually 10 to 30 years) unless the policy is renewed. There is typically no cash value, savings or investment component of term life insurance. Term life insurance is inexpensive, making it a popular option for those looking to cover temporary life insurance needs (particularly young people). The premiums may increase annually or be constant for a set number of years, after which the premiums will rise. Most term policies can be renewed without evidence of insurability up to a certain age (usually 70). First-to-die or joint term life insurance policies pay proceeds when the first holder dies and these policies are often used as part of buy-sell agreements to fund business purchases by surviving business owners. Second-to-die or survivorship term life insurance pays the face value of the policy upon the death of the second insured and can be used for estate planning purposes.

Whole life insurance – permanent insurance that provides you with lifetime insurance protection as long as the policy premiums are paid as agreed. Unlike term life insurance, there is a cash value component to whole life policies with earnings on this cash value credited to the policyholder. As the cash value builds, it can be invested. The investments are typically made as determined by the life insurance company and not at your own direction as the policy owner. Be careful as permanent life insurance investment options have generally been high-cost and inefficient. One appeal of whole life insurance is that gains in the cash account are tax deferred. Ordinary whole life premiums are level throughout the life of the policy and the face amount of the insurance remains constant. These policies tend to benefit those with lower risk tolerances because the insurance company guarantees a minimum cash value. A policyholder can access loans using the cash account value as collateral. Fees are typically quite a bit higher for whole life insurance policies as compared to term life insurance policies.

Variable life insurance - a type of whole life insurance policy with an investment component. The policy has a cash value account in which the insured can choose from a wide variety of investment options (stocks, bonds, money markets etc.). These investment selections impact the policy's face value which can rise or fall depending on investment performance. Like a whole life policy, the gains in a variable life insurance cash account are tax deferred. A policyholder can access loans using the cash account value as collateral. Generally, death benefits can't fall below a guaranteed minimum. Similar to mutual funds and other types of investments, a variable life insurance policy must be presented with a prospectus. A variable life insurance policy deals with investment risk, so it is considered a securities contract and subject to securities law. Make sure any agent attempting to sell you a variable life insurance contract has a valid state license and an NASD license. Variable life premiums are not fixed as they are with a whole life policy and can be shifted up and down over time within certain limits.

Universal life insurance – although it is similar to a whole life policy in that it builds cash value, universal life provides more flexibility through the ability to pay premiums whenever and in the amount you desire. In a universal life policy, premiums are broken into two parts (i) cost of insurance and (ii) savings component referred to as "cash value". The cash value can be invested, but the investments are restricted to whatever is offered by the insurance company which can vary widely from provider to provider. Any excess portion of the cash value can be used to pay the cost of insurance portion of the premium as well. Universal life policies can either have level death benefits or a portion of the death benefit that incorporates the cash balance causing its value to rise and fall. Although universal life policies allow for flexible premium payments, due to the potential change in policy value, universal life policies may not be appropriate for those on fixed incomes.

Quick Tip: life insurance has been popular with high net worth individuals for a number of reasons including (i) providing liquidity while an illiquid asset such as a business is sold (ii) life insurance proceeds can be kept outside of an estate through the use of an Irrevocable Life Insurance Trust (ILIT).

What are the key aspects of disability insurance policies?

A disability can prove to be a greater financial hardship than premature death due to the increase in expenses that often accompanies your loss of income. To protect yourself against this type of situation, disability income insurance provides benefits in the form of periodic payments if you are unable to work as the result of sickness or accidental injury. If the disability arises from a work-related accident you will generally be paid by worker's compensation and not your disability policy. There is no such thing as a standard disability policy, however disability policies do tend to have a number of common provisions that will impact the amount of premium you will pay.

- Disability insurance makes a distinction between short-term and long-term disability coverage. Short-term disability coverage generally provides coverage for up to two years with income replacement often limited to approximately 60% of weekly wages. Long-term disability coverage generally provides benefits for 2 or more years or until the insured reaches a certain age, typically 65. Long-term disability policies can provide up to 75% - 80% of monthly gross wages.

- How disability is actually defined varies depending on the contract:
  - Own occupation is the inability to engage in one's own occupation (this is the most expensive option).
  - Any occupation is the inability to engage in any occupation, not just your own current occupation.
  - Modified any occupation is the inability to engage in any reasonable. occupation for which you might be suited by education, experience or training or for which one could easily become qualified.
  - The Social Security definition of disability is the most restrictive definition of disability. It defines a mental or physical impairment that prevents the worker from engaging in any substantial gainful employment. The disability

must have lasted for 5 months and be expected to last a total of 12 months or result in the death of the worker.

- The waiting period (elimination period) acts as a deductible by making the insured cover part of the financial loss. Elimination periods can be up to 180 days and the shorter the elimination period, the higher the policy premiums.
- Riders can be included to provide you with residual value if you return to work, but are earning less than you did prior to the disability.
- Generally, if disability benefits are received from an employer-provided policy, benefits will be included in W2 income. If the benefits are from a personally paid policy, the benefits will be excluded from your taxable income.

When evaluating the appropriateness and amount of long-term disability coverage you need, you should take into consideration the following:

- The amount of after-tax replacement income you will need. If the policy has a Social Security offset, consider this in your cash flows. The Social Security offset is a program within the Social Security system that adjusts retirement benefits for people that receive a government-based pension.
- The elimination period, particularly as it relates to the premium you will pay.
- The appropriate definition of disability (for example, a professor should have "own occupation").
- Policies should be non-cancellable or guaranteed renewable.

What types of medical insurance policies are available?

Health insurance covers the cost of an insured individual's medical and surgical expenses. Depending on the type of insurance you have, you may pay for expenses out-of-pocket and be reimbursed or your insurer may make payments directly to a provider such as a clinic, hospital, doctor etc. Understanding the basics of your health insurance options will enable you to make more informed decisions regarding your health coverage and financial life.

The Obama Administration introduced legislation making it mandatory for all U.S. citizens to have some form of health insurance or face a monetary penalty. Among numerous other changes, this new legislation keeps plans from rejecting those with pre-existing conditions and allows young people to stay on their parent's healthcare plans for longer. The rules regarding your health insurance can periodically change so make sure to check in with your insurance provider about any policy changes.

Broadly speaking, there are two types of health insurance (i) private health insurance - this form of health insurance is provided to the majority of Americans through their employers (ii) public (government) health insurance - examples of which include Medicare, a federal social insurance for those over age 65 and Medicaid, a form of insurance for those with low enough incomes to qualify. We review public health insurance, particularly Medicare later is this book, but here we look at the key types of private insurance plans you will want to be familiar with. Before reviewing the actual plans, there is certain terminology you will want to be familiar with:

- Deductibles are payments that must be made prior to the application of insurance coverage. Deductibles are generally for a stated dollar amount and period. Deductibles can apply to either an individual or a family.

- Co-payments are amounts an insured must pay to receive certain covered services. These are typically a nominal amount such as a $10 co-payment for a doctor's visit.

- Coinsurance is the percentage paid by the insurer and the insured for claims after the deductible is satisfied and before a stop-loss limit is reached. In an 80/20 coinsurance arrangement, the insured must pay 20% of covered expenses after satisfying the deductible.

- A stop-loss limit is the dollar amount of covered benefits to which the coinsurance provision is applied. Note this amount does not include the deductible and once a stop-loss limit is reached, the insurer pays 100% of the expenses.

- The Breakpoint is the dollar amount of covered expenses after which the insurer pays 100% up to the maximum limit of the policy.

The key types of private health insurance plans include:

Indemnity Plans – as the insured, you can choose any doctor you wish. The doctor, hospital or insured submits a claim for reimbursement to the health insurance company. You will only be reimbursed according to the services listed in the plan "Benefit Summary". Indemnity plans cover a certain percentage (for example 80%) of the costs deemed "reasonable and customary" by the plan in the form of coinsurance. Anything above this "reasonable and customary" level will be covered by the insured. This can make the costs of this type of plan quite burdensome. In addition, indemnity plans can have lifetime expense limits that can make them less appealing.

Health Maintenance Organizations (HMOs) – these plans deliver care directly to you as the insured. You in turn pay the HMO a monthly premium instead of paying for each individual service received. Typically you will select a primary care physician affiliated with the HMO that will coordinate your care and provide all recommendations for specialists. In most cases, coverage will only be provided with such a recommendation and if the specialist is within the provider network. This system helps to lower HMO premium costs. Small co-payments will be required for medical services.

Preferred Provider Organization (PPOs) – you can see any doctor you would like as part of this type of plan (more flexible than HMO), but the amount of required co-payment is dependent on if the doctor is in the PPOs network. If the doctor or service provider is not in the PPO network, the co-payments and coinsurance will be higher than if they are in the PPO network. As part of a PPO, you will have to cover certain expenses in the form of a deductible prior to the reimbursement of any expenses.

Point-of-Service Plans (POS Plans) – combines the characteristics of an HMO and PPO plan. This allows you more flexibility in receiving medical care, but POS plans are usually more expensive than HMO and PPO plans as a result of this flexibility. A POS will allow you to coordinate your medical care through a general practitioner (like an HMO) or go directly to the service provider (like a PPO). How you approach the medical service provider (physician recommendation, no recommendation, in-network, out-of-network) will determine the co-payments, coinsurance and any excess costs you will need to cover. You will often be subject to a deductible as part of a POS plan.

Health Savings Accounts (HSAs) – a Health Savings Account (HSA) can be used with a high-deductible retirement plan. High-deductible retirement plans can take multiple forms including HMOs and PPOs. The key for a high deductible plan is the required deductible. For an individual, the deductible must be at least $1,300, but not more than $6,550. For a family the deductible must be at least $2,600, but not more than $13,100. To make up for these high out-of-pocket costs prior to coverage, insured participants are given the ability to contribute to an

HSA. HSAs are tax-advantaged accounts (tax-free growth of gains) that allow for tax-free withdrawals if the proceeds are used for qualified expenses.

How can businesses use life insurance and health insurance benefits?

Group life and health insurance plans are used by many employers to help compensate and retain their employees. Whether you are an employer or an employee you should understand these insurance and health benefits to make sure you are making the right decisions regarding your options.

Group term life - insurance premiums up to the first $50,000 of coverage paid by an employer are tax-exempt to the employee and deductible by the employer. For any amount of group term life insurance coverage greater than $50,000 a portion of the premium will be included in the employee's W-2 income. Other types of corporate-sponsored insurance policies do not offer the same tax benefits to the employee and employer as the group term life policy.

Split-dollar life insurance - employer and employee share the costs and benefits of the life insurance policy. Typically, the employer will pay the part of the annual premium equivalent to the increase in the cash surrender value of the insurance policy. If the insured employee dies, the employer will recover the premiums it has paid, while the balance of the policy proceeds will be received by the beneficiary named by the deceased employee.

"Cafeteria" insurance benefit plans - allows employees, within limits, to choose their own form of benefits. The plan must include a cash option in which you can receive cash in lieu of non-cash benefits of equal value. This type of plan can be expensive for the employer and complex to administer, but allows employees to "shop" for the best mix of benefits. Cafeteria plans can offer benefits such as group term life insurance and health savings accounts (HSAs).

Flexible Spending Accounts (FSAs) - can be used for the reimbursement of certain qualified employee expenses. FSAs are typically funded by voluntary pre-tax salary reductions, but sometimes can receive employer contributions as well. Although FSAs can offer significant tax benefits to the employee, these accounts can be complex to administer. There are two common types of FSAs (i) Health FSAs allow for the annual reimbursement of medical expenses up to $2,650 and (ii) Dependent Care assistance FSAs allow for a maximum of $5,000 salary reduction for the coverage of dependent care (child care). You typically must use the funds in your FSA prior to year-end, but some employers allow for either a 2 ½ month grace period or a $500 rollover.

Be sure to inquire with your employer regarding any corporate insurance benefits that are available to you.

What are the key aspects of a homeowner's insurance policy?

Homeowner's insurance can cover numerous items associated with your home, from the home itself to the contents of your home. Some types of homeowner's insurance may cover all "perils" except for "exclusions" such as natural disasters, war etc. Other types of homeowner's insurance will only cover "perils" that are specifically named.

When thinking about your homeowner's insurance, the eight general homeowner's insurance exclusions include:

Eight General Homeoners Exclusions	
War	Power Failure
Neglect	Ordinance of Law
Water Damage	International Law
Earth Movement	Nuclear Hazard

Other homeowner's policies specify the perils they provide coverage for. A peril is a specific risk or cause of loss. The 12 basic named perils include:

Twelve Basic Named Perils	
Fire	Aircraft
Lightening	Vehicles
Windstorm	Smoke
Hail	Vandals
Riot or Civil Commotion	Explosions
Theft	Volcanic Eruption

Home insurance policies can have six broad named perils that the policy will cover in addition to the 12 basic named perils. These 6 broad perils include:

Six Broad Named Perils	
Falling Objects	Accident caused by A/C or appliance
Weights of ice, snow and sleet	Freezing of plumbing caused by A/C or appliance
Accidental discharge of water or steam	Sudden and accidental damage from electric current

What homeowner's insurance policies are available?

Each homeowner's policy is divided into two sections, Section I is coverage for property and use of property while Section II is coverage for liability and medical expenses. Section I of each policy is divided into five separate parts; Part A covers the dwelling, Part B covers other structures, Part C covers personal property and Part D covers loss of use. There is another part of Section I that provides additional coverage for the removal of debris, damage to trees and credit card loss.

There are four standard homeowner insurance policy forms. The summaries below are meant strictly as guidance and you should do your own research on homeowner's insurance. There are two additional policies that cover condominium owners and those renting a residence. You should inquire with an insurance or financial professional if these situations apply to you.

- **HO-2 (Broad Form)**: Covers perils 1 – 18 for both home and property. Amount recovered for home is based on replacement cost. Detached buildings are covered for 10% of the insurance on the home, personal property is covered for 50% of the insurance on the home. Loss of use and/or additional living expense is covered for 20% of the insurance of the home.

- **HO-3 (Special Form)**: Covers all perils except those specifically excluded. Perils 1 – 18 are covered for personal property. Amount recovered for home is based on replacement cost. Detached buildings are covered for 10% of the insurance on the home, personal property is covered for 50% of the insurance on the home. Loss of use and/or additional living expense is covered for 20% of the insurance of the home.

- **HO-5 (Comprehensive Form):** Covers all perils except those specifically excluded on both home and property. Amount recovered for home is based on replacement cost. Detached buildings are covered for 10% of the insurance on the home, personal property is covered for 50% of the insurance on the home. Loss of use and/or additional living expense is covered for 20% of the insurance of the home.

- **HO-8 (For Older Homes):** Covers perils 1 – 12. Amount recovered for home is based on cash value. Detached buildings are covered for 10% of the insurance on the home, personal property is covered for 50% of the insurance on the home and loss of use and/or additional living expense is covered for 10 % of the insurance on the home.

Quick Tip: HO-3 (Special Form) and HO-5 (Comprehensive Form) provide you the most coverage as a homeowner, be sure to check with your agent or broker before straying from either of these types of coverage.

What are the key aspects of an automotive insurance policy?

Vehicle insurance is designed to cover the risk of financial liability or loss of a motor vehicle if you are involved in a collision resulting in property damage or physical damage. As the policy owner, you will pay the insurance company a premium. This premium is determined by the type of vehicle you own, your age and gender, your driving history and your geographic location among other factors. Once your coverage is in force, the insurer will provide you with an insurance card to be used as your proof of insurance.

It is more than likely you will receive your automotive coverage through a Personal Auto Policy (PAP). A PAP is a package insurance policy that provides coverage for the losses that result from legal liability, injury to you or loss of an automobile. You can be protected by different levels of coverage depending on the policy you purchase. Often your PAP will take the form of "split coverage" ex. $100/$300/$100. The first two values in the split policy are thresholds for medical coverage, meaning the policy will pay up to $100,000 of medical expenses per person and up to $300,000 of medical expenses in total. The final number in the split policy covers property damage which includes your vehicle or anything you damage as a result of an accident. Instead of "split coverage", your property damage liability coverage and bodily injury coverage can be combined into one single limit.

Other elements of an automotive insurance policy you should look into include "other than collision coverage" and uninsured/underinsured coverage. "Other than collision coverage", often known as comprehensive coverage, relates to damage to a vehicle by incidents not considered a collision such as fire, theft, vandalism, weather or animal impact. Uninsured or underinsured coverage applies if the at-fault party either does not have insurance or does not have enough insurance to cover all liabilities.

Most of the time your automotive policy will cover you as the policy owner, residents of your home or anyone with permission to drive the vehicle. We provide you with a summary of your PAP, but be sure to inquire with your insurance provider with any questions and to make sure you have the correct coverage. In addition, to cover any liabilities above the limits of your PAP (or other insurance policies), you should explore an Umbrella insurance policy which we address in the following question.

Should I have an Umbrella Insurance Policy?

Umbrella insurance is a form of liability insurance that supplements your other basic liability policies, such as your auto and home (renters) insurance. An umbrella liability policy has a much higher coverage limit and goes above and beyond claims against your home and auto. Umbrella policies also provide a broader form of coverage and can help cover legal fees, false arrest, libel, and slander. The purpose of your umbrella policy is to protect your assets from an unforeseen event, such as an accident in which you are held responsible for damages or bodily injuries. If another party files a lawsuit against you, your umbrella coverage will pay for the damages you're legally responsible for up to the policy limit.

Your umbrella insurance can come into play if you are found liable and need to pay damages, or if you are sued and need to pay for your legal defense. An umbrella policy only pays once your basic liability limits have been exhausted. For instance, if the maximum coverage provided by your automotive policy is $300,000 and you are sued for more than $300,000, your umbrella policy will cover this excess liability (up to the umbrella policy limit).

Coverage for an umbrella policy is much cheaper than your home and automotive insurance and premiums typically start at $150-$200 annually for a $1 million policy. Your premium will increase if you decide to increase your umbrella coverage. However, getting twice the amount of coverage (for instance, increasing a $1 million policy limit to $2 million) will not usually double the cost of your premium.

An umbrella insurance policy is especially important for high net worth individuals to make sure the value of their assets is protected above and beyond their basic liability coverage. You will want to consider not only your current assets when deciding how much umbrella insurance you need, but the value of your future income as well. Umbrella policies are common and can be obtained through most insurance providers. Speak with a trusted financial advisor or insurance professional to assess your specific risk factors and determine how to best protect your assets through the use of an umbrella policy.

Further Resources

- **www.naic.org/index_consumer.htm** – this is the National Association of Insurance Commissioners website. The "Consumer" section of this website is very informative, particularly the "Uinsure" subsection. Be sure to download the NAIC Consumer Guides on Home, Auto, Health and Life insurance.

- **www.iii.org** – website of the Insurance Information Institute. The "Topics" section of the website has great unbiased information meant to answer common questions on all types of insurance policies including Life, Homeowners, Automotive, Disability etc.

- **www.lifehealthpro.com** – website is designed for insurance agents and brokers, but has a good deal of useful information in article format for consumers, particularly on life and health insurance policies.

- **www.nolo.com** – in the "Get Informed" section there is a section on "Personal Finance" that contains good information on life insurance. Information is more legal-centric with references to how life insurance relates to beneficiaries and inheritance.

Books:

Reavis, Marshall Wilson III. *Insurance: Concepts & Coverage: Property, Liability, Life, Health and Risk Management*. Insurance Education Publishers, LLC. 2012. Provides an everyday approach to the insurance industry and information on how to examine property, liability, life and health insurance programs. Gives the basics on how to set up your own risk management program.

Chapter 5: Planning for Retirement

✓ Estimate the amount you will need to fund retirement. Figure out the annual savings needed to meet this goal.

✓ Do you know the type of retirement plan your employer offers? Are you enrolled in your employer's retirement plan? Familiarize yourself with the characteristics of the plan.

✓ Figure out if you may be eligible to set up and contribute to other types of retirement plans such as Individual Retirement Accounts (IRAs) or a Roth IRA.

✓ When it comes time to make withdrawals or take distributions from your retirement plan(s), understand the distribution rules and tax implications.

If retirement is part of your financial plan, start saving now if you haven't already. Saving for retirement is especially complex because you will be saving for (and spending on) numerous other goals in the interim. Then, once you get to your retirement years, you will still have plenty of time and life events left to fund. When planning for retirement, you should start by answering basic questions such as "When do I want to retire?" "Where do I want to live in retirement?" "What does my retired lifestyle look like?". You should come up with an estimate of the amount of money you will need in retirement and the savings it will take to get there. This estimate is especially challenging with factors like escalating health care costs and longer life expectancies. A budget, no matter how preliminary, which identifies future income sources (Social Security, retirement plan withdrawals) and expenses (healthcare costs, housing etc.) will prove helpful with your retirement estimates. In addition to a budget, you should understand the various resources you can use to save for retirement through your employer or on your own. Whether you are still contributing to a retirement plan or have already started making withdrawals from your plan in retirement, it is important that you familiarize yourself with characteristics of the various account types as well as the distribution rules and tax regulations that apply to each.

Quick Tip: you can construct a retirement budget yourself, or try out an online site such a Mint.com or BudgetTracker.com. Some banks have this service available for you as well. The important thing is not how you make a budget, just that you construct one! There are plenty of free online retirement calculators you can use to estimate your retirement needs including those provided by Fidelity and Schwab.

What are the different types of retirement plans?

To encourage retirement savings, the U.S. government created a variety of tax-favored retirement plans and strategies. Retirement plans come in numerous forms and characteristics can overlap between plan types. Retirement plans can be either "Qualified" or "Tax-Advantaged". A retirement plan is considered Qualified because it provides formal tax advantages under the Internal Revenue Code (IRC) to both employers and employees. Tax-Advantaged plans are similar in appearance to Qualified Plans, but are not technically required by ERISA (the body of laws that regulate employee benefit plans) to follow U.S. Tax Code 401(a) under the IRC. As opposed to Qualified Plans, which are offered by your employer, you can set up many Tax-Advantaged plans yourself. In this chapter we will go through some of the more common/popular types of retirement plans. If your plan type or a plan type you are interested in is not covered, inquire with your employer, a financial advisor, or even the IRS which has very good information on retirement plans.

Summary of Retirement Plans		
Qualified Retirement Plans		**Other Tax-Advantaged Retirement Plans**
Pension Plans	**Profit-Sharing**	
• Defined Benefit Plan[DB]	• Traditional Profit-Sharing Plan	• Traditional IRAs
• Cash Balance Plan[DB]	• 401(k) Plans	• Roth IRAs
• DB(k) Plan[DB]	• Simple 401(k)	• SIMPLE IRAs
• Target Benefit Plan	• Thrift Plans	• SEP plans
• Money Purchase Plan	• Age-based Profit-sharing Plan	• Section 457 plans

"DB" represents Defined Benefit Plans. All other Qualified Retirement Plans are Defined Contribution Plans. **Source:** *Certified Financial Planner* ® website, www.cfp.net.

When they offer a Qualified retirement plan, an employer can receive immediate tax deductibility (a reduction in an employer's income subject to tax) for all contributions they make to a Qualified retirement plan on behalf of employees. Typically, the amount an employer can deduct for such contributions is limited to 25% of total payroll. As an employee, you are not taxed on contributions you make to a Qualified retirement plan and both your initial contributions and the earnings on these contributions are not taxed until you withdraw them. This allows the earnings on the contributions you make to your plan, that would normally be taxed, to grow tax-deferred until withdrawal (unless the plan is a Roth which is discussed later in this chapter). This concept is referred to as compound growth and is one of the most powerful tools you have when saving for retirement (see "Quick Tip"). Ideally distributions from your Qualified retirement account will not occur until you have retired and are subject to a lower ordinary income tax bracket. This is because when you retire, any withdrawals you take from your Qualified retirement plan will hypothetically be subject to a much lower income tax rate because you will have ceased earning taxable income.

As shown in the prior exhibit, Qualified retirement plans can either be pension plans or profit-sharing plans. A pension plan is the employer's promise to pay employees a specified benefit at retirement. Pension plans require mandatory annual contributions by an employer based on an actuarial formula intended to meet future benefits. These annual contributions must be made regardless of the employer's profitability. The traditional defined benefit pension plan is the most well-known known pension plan, but in recent years, other types of plans such as Cash Balance Plans, Target Benefit Plans and DB(k) plans have been developed with the intention of making employer funding requirements less difficult to meet.

Unlike pension plans, which require an employer to fund a set retirement benefit for participants, profit-sharing plans promise no set benefit, and offer employees only the opportunity to defer taxes on all employer and employee contributions to the retirement plan. This means the value of your account at retirement is not known and an employer is not obligated to meet any set benefit level for you. Unlike pension plans, annual funding is not required for profit-sharing plans, but must be "substantial and recurring" according to the IRS. One of the most familiar profit-sharing plans is the 401(k) plan which allows participants to directly defer salary into their own retirement accounts.

Qualified pension plans and qualified profit-sharing plans are often categorized as either defined benefit plans or defined contribution plans. If you refer to the "Summary of Retirement Plans" exhibit, Defined Benefit Plans, Cash Balance Plans and DB(k) Plans are categorized as defined benefit plans while all remaining plans are categorized as defined contribution plans. Defined benefit plans are a type of pension plan that specifies a formula to determine future participant benefits based on variables such as years of service and level of salary. This tends to favor older and higher-paid plan participants. Defined benefit plans have become less popular over time as more employers have had trouble meeting burdensome contribution requirements. Calculating a defined benefit formula requires actuarial work and increases the cost of maintaining these plans. Defined benefit plans commingle all participant accounts into one large pool which is then used to fund future benefits as employees retire. All investment risk in defined benefit plans is borne by the employer and there are specific rules that must be followed in the event of a funding shortfall.

In a defined contribution plan, the employer establishes and maintains individual accounts for each plan participant as opposed to one commingled account in a defined benefit plan. The employer does not guarantee the amount of benefit a participant will receive as part of a defined contribution plan, but an employer must make regular contributions to the plan under a specified formula. Investment risk in a defined contribution plan is borne by the employee.

Although not technically "Qualified", other types of retirement plans still offer substantial tax advantages. These Tax-Advantaged plans promise to pay the participant an accumulated plan balance at retirement, the value of which will not be known until retirement. The employee and not the employer is ultimately responsible for investment performance and the value of the retirement plan account balance. The contribution and distribution rules for these Tax-

Advantaged plans are very similar to those of Qualified plans. Some of these Tax-Advantaged plans you can set up and fund yourself, such as an Individual Retirement Account (IRA) or Roth IRA, while other Tax-Advantaged plans will be set up in conjunction with an employer, such as a Simplified Employer Pension (SEP) Plan or 403(b) plan.

Quick Tip: a one-time $5,000 investment made at age 20 that earns an 8% annual return will grow to just under $160,000 by the time you reach age 65. If a 20% annual tax rate on all earnings is assumed the value you receive at 65 falls to roughly $69,000. The value of tax-deferral is $90,000. This is the power of compound, tax-deferred growth.

What rules and regulations must a retirement plan follow to be considered Qualified?

In exchange for the tax advantages discussed earlier (employer tax deductibility and employee tax deferral), Qualified retirement plans must adhere to certain rules and regulations as dictated by the Internal Revenue Service (IRS) and Department of Labor (DOL). Many of these rules and regulations are contained in the federal legislation laid out by the Employment Retirement Income Security Act (ERISA) and further detail on individual retirement plans can be found in plan documents such as the Summary Plan Document (SPD). An employer is required to provide you a copy of the SPD annually. These requirements are very important for employers to understand as failure to adhere to them can result in fines or even the disqualification of the plan. As an employee, you should be familiar with these requirements because they ensure the plan in which you are enrolled is fair and well run. A Qualified plan must meet ERISA requirements with respect to:

- – Vesting
- – Coverage
- – Participation
- – Reporting and Disclosure
- – Fiduciary Requirements

Vesting is the process by which you as a plan participant become entitled to ownership of an account value in a Qualified plan. Defined benefit plans must vest at least as rapidly as the below schedule:

Years of Service	Vested Percentage
3	20%
4	40%
5	60%
6	80%
7 or more	100%

If cliff-vesting is used in a defined benefit plan, five-year cliff vesting must be used. This means that after five years, participants have complete 100% access to their benefits.

A defined contribution plan must vest at least as rapidly as the below schedule:

Years of Service	Vested Percentage
2	20%
3	40%
4	60%
5	80%
6 or more	100%

If cliff-vesting is used in a defined contribution plan, three-year cliff vesting must be used so that after three years participants have full access to their assets. An employer that offers either type of plan, can opt for a less stringent vesting schedule, but can't have a more stringent vesting schedule.

All Qualified plans must pass **coverage and participation** tests to ensure plans do not favor a certain category of employee, particularly highly paid employees or management. The first of these tests is called "the general rule test" which requires that an employer cover at least 70% of all non-excludable, non-highly compensated employees (NHCE). For testing purposes, a highly compensated employee (HCE) is considered to be either (i) a 5% owner at any time during the current or preceding year or (ii) received compensation greater than $120,000 during the prior year. If a Qualified plan does not meet the general rule test, there are two other tests it can meet, the Ratio Percentage Test or the Average Benefits Percentage Test to satisfy ERISA coverage. This tests can be complex, so refer to a financial advisor or tax expert for details.

Defined benefit plans (but not defined contribution plans) then must pass an additional coverage test called "the 50/40 test". The 50/40 test requires defined benefit plans to cover the lesser of:

a. 50 employees

b. 40% or more of all non-excludable employees

For example, under the 50/40 test, if a company has 1,000 employees, 50 must be covered by the defined benefit plan. If the company has 100 employees, at least 40 must be covered.

If benefits are too favorable for a certain group of employees, Qualified plans may be considered "top-heavy". A plan is "top-heavy" if the present value of key employee accrued benefits is greater than 60% of all accrued benefits in a Qualified plan. If the account values for key employees are greater than 60% of all account values for a defined contribution plan, the plan is considered "top-heavy". A key employee is defined as (i) an officer with compensation in excess of $170,000 (ii) a greater than 5% owner or (iii) a greater than 1% owner with compensation over a certain threshold set by the IRS. To avoid favoring highly compensated employees, if a qualified plan is "top heavy" certain changes and modifications must be made for the plan to remain qualified. If the plan is "top heavy", the plan must move to a more advantageous and rapid vesting schedule.

There are both **service and age requirements** needed to participate in a Qualified plan. A participant must be both 21 years of age and have one year of service at the employer (as represented by 1,000 hours). A Qualified plan can increase the service requirement period to two years, but in that case, the plan must provide immediate vesting (401(k)'s can't require two years of service). Once a participant meets eligibility requirements, plan enrollment must occur at the next available entrance date. An eligible participant can't be required to wait more than 6 months to enroll, therefore a Qualified plan must have at least 2 entrance dates each year.

To satisfy **reporting and disclosure requirements**, employers must provide you as a plan participant with certain documents. You may find these documents useful in monitoring and learning more about your Qualified retirement plan. These documents include the Form 5500 annual report which contains detailed financial/actuarial information on the Qualified plan and the Summary Plan Description (SPD) which gives an overview of the plan and its attributes.

As a participant you should be familiar with your plan's testing requirements, and aware that this testing exists to ensure your plan is fair to all participants. Realize that the responsibility of testing falls on your employer, your employer's financial advisor and the "Third Party Administrator" though.

A Qualified plan must specifically designate a **fiduciary** or fiduciaries responsible for the administration and management of the plan. ERISA obligations require the fiduciary to exercise the care, skill and diligence of a prudent person acting solely in the interest of plan participants and beneficiaries. In addition, ERISA requires a fiduciary to diversify the plan's assets, act in accordance with the plan's provisions and refrain from acts forbidden under the law. Fiduciary standards relate to procedure and not performance, meaning that a fiduciary's success is not necessarily measured by returns. Other individuals beyond the named fiduciary may acquire fiduciary obligations. These individuals can include corporate officers and directors, plan administrators, bank trustees, the investment committee, investment advisors and those that select other fiduciaries.

What are the characteristics of a Qualified pension plan?

We will review traditional defined benefit plans in detail here, however other types of pension plans such as Cash Balance Pension plans, Money Purchase Pension plans, DB(k) plans and Target Balance plans have become more popular and are defined in the glossary of this book. If you need further information on these types of pension plans you can ask your employer, a financial advisor or the Internal Revenue Service (IRS).

The object of a **traditional defined benefit plan** is to provide a defined level of income upon retirement to each plan participant. As discussed previously, employer contributions to a traditional defined benefit plan are deductible for income tax purposes when made and taxation to the employee is deferred until the employee receives distribution of retirement plan funds. Annual contributions are allowed up to an amount actuarially determined to fund future benefits. For 2018, these future annual actuarial benefits can't exceed the lesser of (i) 100% of participant's compensation averaged over the 3 highest years and (ii) $220,000. These thresholds allow for greater contributions than other types of Qualified plans, particularly profit-sharing plans. Defined benefit plan contribution formulas can take multiple forms including a flat dollar formula, a flat percentage formula (a uniform percentage applied to compensation), or a unit credit formula where the percentage applied to participant compensation is based on years of service. The average earnings used in these formulas can be based on average earnings over a whole career or over the final few years, which is more beneficial for older plan participants.

An employer should have steady cash flows to implement a traditional defined benefit plan as annual plan funding is mandatory. If a traditional defined benefit plan is terminated without sufficient assets to pay accrued benefits, the Pension Benefit Guaranty Corporation (PBGC) is liable for this unfunded balance (to a limited extent). The PBGC is an independent agency of the United States government created by ERISA to encourage the continuation and maintenance of voluntary private defined benefit pension plans. This PBGC insurance is provided only for defined benefit plans and is financed through premiums paid by the employer.

Mandatory funding and the actuarial expense of maintaining traditional defined pension plans have made these plans less popular over time and given rise to other types of pension plans that are easier for employers to fund and manage including Cash Balance Pension plans, Money Purchase Pension plans, DB(k) plans and Target Balance plans. These newer pension plans still allow for advantageous contribution levels, but are much more transparent and manageable than a traditional defined benefit plan when it comes to predictability of cash flows. Further information on these newer types of pension plans is contained in the glossary of this book.

What are the characteristics of Qualified profit-sharing plans?

As we did previously with pension plans, in this section we look at some of the more common types of Qualified profit-sharing plans. If the profit-sharing plan you're interested in isn't addressed here, definitely contact your employer, a financial advisor or the Internal Revenue Service (IRS) about the plan in question.

A **profit-sharing plan** is the legal promise to defer taxes on employer and employee contributions to the plan. Unlike pension plans, there are no mandatory funding requirements as part of a profit-sharing plan. Contributions can be either at the employer's discretion or based on a formula such as a percentage of participant salary. Total annual additions to a profit-sharing plan are limited to the lesser of 100% of employee compensation or $55,000. This $55,000 can be divided into an $18,500 maximum salary deferral you can make yourself as an employee and $36,500 that can be provided by your employer in the form of a match (this match is what most of us are used to ex. if I contribute X%, my employer will provide a match of Y%), safe harbor contribution or profit-sharing. A participant can make an additional "catch-up" contribution of $6,000 to a profit-sharing plan if they are 50 years old or older. Any excess contributions will result in a 10% excise tax. Employers can deduct a maximum of 25% of total employee compensation.

Unlike pension plans, which have stringent annual contribution requirements, profit-sharing plans allow more contribution flexibility. An employer can even forego contributions during years of low profitability. Despite this flexibility, a discretionary contribution must be considered substantial and recurring according to IRS standards, which is typically viewed as three of every five years. Each employee has an individual account as part of a profit-sharing plan, and the plan benefit consists of the amount accumulated in the participant's account at retirement. The value of participant accounts is not guaranteed and is dependent on investment performance. This is contrary to pension plans where the employer instead of the employee is responsible for investment performance. ERISA requires profit-sharing plans to offer at least three investment options, a money market fund, a bond fund, and a stock fund. In addition, ERISA requires a certain level of participant education be provided.

The most popular profit-sharing plan is known as a **401(k) plan**. A 401(k) plan is a specific type of profit-sharing plan typically provided by an employer that gives you the option to contribute before-tax compensation to the plan. This choice is called an "elective-deferral". The maximum elective deferral a participant can make into a 401(k) plan is $18,500 annually with an additional $6,000 "catch-up" for participants age 50 or older. An employer can make contributions to a participant's account as well. These employer contributions often take the form of a formula matching contribution and can include a profit-sharing element as well. In 2018, the maximum value of the combined employee deferral and employer contribution can't exceed $55,000 ($61,000 including the $6,000 "catch-up" for participants over 50).

Solo 401(k) plans are the most popular types of self-employed retirement plans. Self-employed qualified plans are extremely similar to traditional 401(k) plans with two primary differences (i) self-employed individuals must calculate their maximum retirement plan contribution on the basis of self-employment income instead of W-2 income (ii) a net contribution rate is applied to earned self-employed income to determine annual contributions. This net contribution rate can be found in the "Self-Employed Person's Retirement Plan Contribution Rate Table" on the IRS website.

A 401(k) plan must satisfy certain nondiscriminatory coverage tests so that Highly Compensated Employees (HCEs) are not favored over Non-Highly Compensated Employees (NHCEs). The nondiscriminatory coverage tests relate to both employee deferrals (Actual Deferral Percentage Test) and employer contributions (Actual Contribution Percentage Test).

If ADP or ACP of NHC is:	Maximum ADP or ACP of HC is:
≤ 2%	2x ADP or ACP of NHC
2% - 8%	2% + ADP or ACP of NHC
≥ 8%	1.25 x ADP or ACP of NHC

If a plan fails the non-discriminatory coverage tests it has two available corrective actions. The first is a corrective distribution made reducing the ADP or ACP of HCEs, the second is an additional non-elective contribution made to all NHCEs. The correction must be made within 2 ½ months of the end of the year or the employer must pay a 10% excise tax. As a participant it is good to understand that the purpose of this testing is to ensure your retirement plan is fair to all participants, but that testing is ultimately the responsibility of your employer (the plan sponsor).

As discussed, a profit sharing/401(k) plan must satisfy certain non-discrimination requirements. In 1996 though, the Small Business Job Protection Act provided employer's sponsoring 401(k) plans with a simplified alternative known as a **Safe Harbor plan.** A Safe Harbor retirement plan automatically passes the ADP, ACP and "top-heavy" testing, allowing business owners to maximize their plan contributions. In exchange for not having to pass non-discriminatory testing, employers must meet certain contribution requirements. These requirements can be met in a number of ways. An employer can match 100% of the first 3% and 50% of the next 2% an employee contributes to the plan. As an alternative, the employer can make a 3% non-elective contribution to each plan participant regardless of if the participant makes their own deferral contribution. Employers can use a newer type of Safe Harbor alternative called a Qualified Automatic

Contribution Arrangement (QACA). A QACA must allow, unless a participant elects otherwise, to have a qualified percentage of compensation deferred on the participant's behalf. The qualified percentage can't exceed 10% and must be equal to at least 3% in year one and increase by 1% thereafter until reaching 6% in year four.

A **Savings Incentive Match Plan for Employees (SIMPLE) 401(k)** is available to employers that do not maintain another employer-sponsored plan. To offer a SIMPLE an employer must have 100 or fewer employees that earned at least $5,000 during the fiscal year. An employer has a 2 year grace period to maintain a SIMPLE plan even if the eligible number of participants exceeds 100. A SIMPLE is actually a type of safe harbor plan and not subject to the non-discrimination rules (ADP, ACP and "top-heavy"). This means the deferrals made by Highly Compensated Employees (HCEs) are not limited by the deferrals made by Non-Highly Compensated Employees (NHCEs). To become eligible for a SIMPLE plan, a participant must have earned at least $5,000 during 2 preceding years and be reasonably expected to earn $5,000 or more during the current year. The elective deferral limits for a SIMPLE are less than for a traditional 401(k) and contributions are automatically 100% vested. Employees can contribute up to $12,500 annually to a SIMPLE in 2018 and participants over 50 years old can make a "catch-up" contribution of $3,000 each year. An employer that offers a SIMPLE plan can't offer any other types of retirement plans.

Employer matching contributions to a SIMPLE 401(k) are limited to 3% of the employee's annual total salary. As an alternative to this match, an employer can make a non-elective contribution to all eligible employees (not just those participants contributing to the plan) equal to 2% of compensation. Early distributions (withdrawals) from a SIMPLE 401(k) are subject to a 25% penalty if made within the first 2 years of the plan while you are under the age of 59 1/2. If an early distribution is taken after 2 years, the participant may still face a 10% penalty unless the distribution qualifies for an exemption.

As outlined in the Retirement Plan Summary exhibit, there are a number of other profit-sharing plans available to you including stock bonus plans, Employee Stock Ownership Plans (ESOPs) and Savings/Thrift plans among others. These plans are defined in the glossary of this book, or you can contact your employer, a financial advisor or the Internal Revenue Service (IRS) for further detail.

What other Tax-Advantaged retirement plans are available?

One of the greatest advantages when saving for retirement are the tax benefits you receive on your investments. Although they may not technically be considered Qualified, there are many other types of accounts that can offer you significant tax advantages. Certain accounts, such as an Individual Retirement Account (IRA) or a Roth IRA you can easily set up and contribute to yourself, while other plans are offered through an employer such as a SEP plan, or a Section 403(b) plan.

A **traditional IRA** allows for tax-deductible investments meaning that tax will not be applied until withdrawals are made from the IRA later in your life. In 2018 annual investor contributions to an IRA are limited to $5,500 with an additional $1,000 "catch-up" contribution allowed if you are over 50 years old. You can set up a traditional IRA if you have taxable compensation and are younger than age 70 ½. Your ability to deduct contributions to a traditional IRA (thus lowering your income subject to tax) is dependent on your participation in any another retirement plan, and your Modified Adjusted Gross Income (MAGI). For taxpayers who are not active participants in a Qualified Plan, SEP, SIMPLE, or 403(b) (note a Section 457 plan is not considered for the purposes of IRA deductibility), contributions to an IRA are fully deductible regardless of MAGI. For taxpayers who are active participants in one of these retirement plans, the deduction for IRA contributions is phased out from MAGI levels of $63,000 to $73,000 for single tax filers, MAGI levels of $101,000 to $121,000 for married couples filing jointly and $10,000 for married couples filing separately. When only one spouse is an active participant in a retirement plan, the MAGI phase out levels for the non-active spouse rises to a range of $189,000 to $199,000.

Non-deductible contributions can still be made to an IRA even if an investor's MAGI exceeds the thresholds. There is a 6% excise tax on excess contributions to an IRA. Annual contributions to an IRA must be made by the due date of your tax return (generally April 15th). An IRA does not allow for either employee loans or the purchase of insurance, which are usually available in 401k plans. You can't make contributions to a traditional IRA past age 70 ½. An IRA can take the form of a Roth IRA allowing investors to make after-tax contributions (not deductible) that can potentially avoid all tax thereafter if applicable rules are followed. Roth IRAs are addressed in further detail later in this chapter.

A **Simplified Employer Pension Plan (SEP)** is a less expensive alternative to a Qualified profit-sharing plan most often used by smaller employers. A SEP is actually an agreement by an employer to contribute on a non-discriminatory basis to IRAs opened and maintained by employees (therefore the employee bears the investment risk). All SEP contributions are made by the employer and there are no elective deferrals allowed by the employee. Employer contributions are made on a non-discriminatory basis (i.e. the same percentage of salary is provided for every employee). An employer can deduct contributions up to the contribution limit. The limit for annual SEP contributions is the lesser of (i) 25% of compensation or (ii) $55,000. A SEP allows no "catch-up" contributions. A 10% excise tax is applied to all excess contributions. SEP plans can be adopted and funded as late as the tax return filing date, including extensions (as opposed to December 31 for most Qualified Plans). Employers are free to make no contribution to a SEP in any given year, but contributions are always fully vested. A SEP plan must cover all employees that are at least age 21 and have worked for the employer during three of the proceeding five years. Contributions don't have to be made on behalf of an employee whose compensation is less than $600 in 2018. An employer can maintain both a SEP and another Qualified Plan, but contributions to the SEP reduce the amount the employer can deduct for contributions to other Qualified Plans.

An employer can establish a **SIMPLE IRA** that is very similar to the SIMPLE 401(k) option described previously in terms of eligibility and contributions. Employers must have 100 or fewer employees that earned at least $5,000 during the fiscal year. Employees can contribute up to $12,500 annually to a SIMPLE IRA in 2018 and participants over 50 years old can make a "catch-up" contribution of $3,000 each year. Employer matching contributions to a SIMPLE IRA are limited to 3% of the employee's annual total salary. Alternatively, the employer can make a non-elective contribution to all eligible employees equal to 2% of compensation. Unlike a SIMPLE 401(k) in which the employer elective deferral match can't be reduced below 3%, with a SIMPLE IRA, the employer can match as little as 1% of employee compensation in two of every five years.

A **Section 403(b) plan**, which is often referred to as a Tax Deferred Annuity (TDA) is used by tax-exempt 501(c)(3) non-for-profit organizations or public schools. Section 403(b) plans do not have to follow ERISA guidelines so are not technically Qualified plans. A 403(b) allows employees to make tax-deferred savings in their own accounts. The "universal availability rule" applies to 403(b) plans. This means that if an employer permits one employee to defer salary into a 403(b) plan, the employer must extend this offer to all employees of the organization. A 403(b) plan must meet at least one of three coverage tests to ensure it does not favor Highly Compensated Employees (HCEs) (i) The ratio test, in which the percentage of non-Highly Compensated Employees (NHCEs) who participate in the plan must be at least 70% of the percentage of HCEs (ii) The percentage test, in which the plan must benefit a minimum of 70% of NHCEs and (iii) the average benefit percentage for non-highly compensated employees must be at least 70% of the average benefit percentage for HCEs.

Like a 401(k), participants can make a maximum annual elective deferral to a 403(b) of up to $18,500 with an additional $6,000 "catch-up" for participants 50 or older. A 403(b) is subject to overall contribution limits of the lesser of 100% of compensation or $55,000 ($61,000 including the over "catch-up"). Although the ADP test does not apply, 403(b) plans must comply with the ACP test for matching contributions. Investment in individual stocks and bonds are not permitted in 403(b) plans. The permitted investments in a 403(b) consist of annuities and mutual funds.

A 403(b) plan allows for a special set of catch-up contributions. Once an employee has completed 15 years of service for an eligible organization the participant may increase their contribution limit to a 403(b) by the lesser of the following (i) $3,000 (ii) $15,000 reduced by amounts previously contributed under this catch-up contribution or (iii) $5,000 multiplied by the employee's years of service less the sum of all prior salary deferrals. These special catch-up contributions must be exhausted prior to the normally allowed catch-up contributions of $6,000 for those participants 50 years old and older. Employees working less than 1,000 hours may be excluded from a 403(b), but all other employees are generally allowed to participate.

A **Section 457 plan** is a non-qualified deferred compensation plan used by state and local government units as well as non-church controlled, tax-exempt organizations. Contributions to these plans are made on a pre-tax basis and funds grow tax deferred. Investment risks are borne by employees that participate in the plan. A Section 457 plan can either be public or private. Public 457 plans are used by both key employees as well as rank and file employees of state and local governments. Plan assets are placed in trust so they are not available to creditors. Private Section 457 plans are used by key and highly-compensated employees of tax-exempt organizations. Plan assets of private 457 plans are not placed in trust and therefore available to satisfy an employer's creditors.

An employee's annual deferrals to a Section 457 plan can't exceed the lesser of $18,500 or 100% of the employee's compensation. Eligible public 457 plans allow participants who have attained age 50 to make a "catch-up" contribution of $6,000 in 2018. Both public and private Section 457 plans allow you as a participant to double the contribution limit in the three years prior to retirement. These excess contributions are limited to prior year deferrals the participant has not taken. During this three-year period when contributions can be doubled the normal age 50 or older "catch-up" rules don't apply.

Quick Tip: You can open an IRA account numerous places for free including Fidelity, Vanguard and TD Ameritrade among others. The process is not difficult, just call up the custodian (another term for companies like Fidelity, Vanguard and TD Ameritrade) or work with an advisor to have them walk you through it.

What is the Roth feature of a retirement plan?

Many of us are familiar with the Roth feature of an IRA, but this feature can be offered by your employer in the form of a Roth 401(k), a Roth 403(b) or a Roth 457 plan as well. Regardless of the type of retirement savings vehicle, the key attribute of a Roth is the tax treatment. A Roth allows investors to make after-tax contributions (not deductible) that can potentially avoid all tax thereafter if all applicable rules are followed.

In 2018, annual investor contributions to a Roth IRA are limited to $5,500 with an additional $1,000 "catch-up" contribution allowed for those over 50 years old. These contribution limits are across both Traditional and Roth IRAs (you can't contribute more than $5,500 in aggregate to both a traditional and Roth IRA).

An investor's ability to make contributions to a Roth IRA is dependent on their MAGI. Roth IRA contributions are phased out at MAGI levels of $189,000 - $199,000 for married couples filing jointly, $120,000 - $135,000 for single filers and $10,000 for married couples filing separately. Remember, for traditional IRAs, your MAGI levels may limit your ability to make deductible contributions, but non-deductible contributions can be made regardless of your MAGI. As long as you have earned income, contributions to a Roth IRA can be made past the age of 70 ½, an important distinction from traditional IRAs which do not allow this. Like Traditional IRAs, you can make contributions to a Roth IRA up to the annual tax filing deadline.

A Roth account is a separate account in a 401(k), 403(b) or governmental 457(b) that holds designated Roth contributions. These Roth contributions are includible in a participant's gross income and thus taxed at your ordinary income tax rates in the year of contribution, but all eligible distributions (including earnings) from the account are tax free. A participant can designate some or all of their elective deferrals as Roth contributions rather than traditional, pre-tax elective deferrals. Organizations offering a Roth account are required to separately track the values in this account. As an employee/participant you can make a maximum deferral contribution to a designated Roth account of $18,500 annually with an additional $6,000 "catch-up" for participants 50 or older. In addition to the contribution to a designated Roth retirement plan, you can make contributions to your IRA or Roth IRA if you qualify. An employer can make matching contributions in addition to your Roth contributions, however only your own designated Roth contributions can be deposited in the actual Roth account. Your employer must allocate their matching contributions into a pre-tax non-Roth account. Note we cover the various regulations that apply when taking distributions from a Roth account later in this chapter.

How do I take distributions from my retirement plan?

Generally, all distributions from retirement plans will be taxed at your ordinary income rate, but there are numerous exceptions to this rule you should be aware of. Retirement plan distributions can be voluntarily made at your request or you may be required to take a distribution from your retirement plan. The taxation of any distribution will be impacted by variables such as the age of the account owner, beneficiary relationships (spouse or non-spouse), type of retirement account and reason for the distribution. Defined benefit plans typically offer participant distributions in the form of an annuity, while profit-sharing plans such as 401(k)s allow for more flexibility as long the participant meets certain requirements, most notably reaching age 59 ½. Distribution rules can vary by plan, so be sure to check with your employer and the Summary Plan Document (SPD) for details.

Taking distributions from your profit-sharing/401(k) plan: While working for an employer, you generally can't take distributions from that employer's qualified retirement plan prior to (i) reaching age 59 ½ (ii) death or (iii) disability. If one of these three requirements is met, you will pay ordinary income tax on the taxable portion of the distribution. The taxable portion is everything aside from the qualified plan's cost basis. Cost basis consists of contributions to a Qualified plan that have already been taxed (after-tax contributions). If none of the three distribution scenarios apply you must be eligible for a "hardship withdrawal". An employer may or may not allow for hardship withdrawals as part of a Qualified plan. In addition, prior to taking a hardship withdrawal, as a participant you must prove that no other resources are available to cover this need. Despite these negatives, a hardship withdrawal can be a better alternative than making a direct withdrawal and potentially disqualifying your plan. If you are considering making a hardship withdrawal, definitely consult with your employer or financial advisor.

A hardship withdrawal can only be taken for one of the following reasons:

- Unexpected medical expenses
- Costs relating to the purchase of a home
- Tuition and related educational fees and expenses
- Payments necessary to prevent eviction from or foreclosure on a home
- Burial or funeral expenses
- Expenses to repair damage to your home

You will pay ordinary income taxes on the taxable portion of these distributions as well as a penalty tax of 10% (penalty only applies to taxable portion of distribution). You may be able to avoid the 10% penalty tax if you qualify for one of the following exceptions:

- You are disabled
- Your medical debt exceeds 7.5% of your Adjusted Gross Income (AGI)
- You are required by court order to give money to a divorced spouse, a child or dependent

For six months after you take a hardship withdrawal you will not be allowed to make contributions to your Qualified plan and you are never allowed to pay back the amount you withdrew. Remember that while in a qualified plan such as a 401(k), your assets are protected from creditors in the event of a bankruptcy filing. For planning purposes, you will want to analyze alternatives to a hardship withdrawal such as a loan from your Qualified plan.

Taking distributions from your IRA or Roth IRA: Like a profit sharing/40(k) plan, you generally can't access funds without penalty in your IRA or Roth IRA unless (i) you reach age 59 ½ (ii) you die or (iii) you become disabled. In the event of these occurrences, you will pay ordinary income tax on all distributions from an IRA, but no tax at all on distributions from a Roth IRA (remember, initial contributions were after-tax) as long as certain requirements are met. We will look at these Roth requirements shortly. You can take distributions from your IRA (including your SEP IRA or SIMPLE IRA) at any time and unlike a profit-sharing/401(k) plan, there is no need to show a hardship to take a distribution. However, your distribution will be includible in your taxable income and it may be subject to a 10% additional tax if you don't meet one of the three exceptions detailed previously. The additional tax is 25% if you take a distribution from your SIMPLE IRA in the first 2 years you participate. There are a few additional wrinkles when accessing funds from an IRA or Roth IRA, so be sure to understand the full impact when contemplating a withdrawal.

In a Traditional IRA, if you are under the age of 59½, you may make taxable, but penalty-free withdrawals from your traditional IRA under certain circumstances including:

- You die and the account value is paid to your beneficiary
- You become disabled
- You use an early withdrawal to pay medical expenses that are more than 10% of your adjusted gross income (AGI)
- You are unemployed and use the early IRA withdrawal to pay for your medical insurance
- You begin substantially equal periodic payments (IRS code section 72(t))
- Your withdrawal is related to a qualified domestic relations order (QDRO)
- Your withdrawal is used to pay qualified higher education expenses
- Your withdrawal is used for a qualified "first-home" purchase (up to $10,000)

You can withdraw contributions you make to a Roth IRA tax and penalty free (remember you've already paid the tax), however if you are under age 59 ½ when you make a Roth IRA withdrawal, you may be subject to taxes and penalties on the earnings in your Roth IRA depending on the amount of time you've held the account.

The key to the avoidance of tax and penalties when it comes to a Roth IRA is the amount of time the account has been open, referred to as the "5 Year Rule". The 5 Year Rule for Roth IRA earnings starts on January 1st of the year you make your first Roth IRA contribution. With no exception, a withdrawal from your Roth IRA prior to meeting the 5 year holding period requirement will result in ordinary income tax on all earnings as well as the 10% penalty tax. If your Roth account does meet the 5 year holding period, the tax and penalties you incur will depend on if you have reached age 59 ½. Remember all taxes and penalties apply only to earnings and not after-tax contributions.

If you are under age 59 ½ and have not met the 5 year holding period the earnings in your account will be subject to ordinary income taxes, but not penalties if:

- You use the withdrawal (up to a $10,000 lifetime maximum) to pay for a first-time home purchase
- You use the withdrawal to pay for qualified education expenses
- You become disabled or pass away
- You use the withdrawal to pay for unreimbursed medical expenses or health insurance if you're unemployed
- The distribution is made in substantially equal periodic payments

If your Roth account does meet the 5-year holding period requirement, you will be subject to neither tax nor penalties on the above exceptions. After age 59 ½ if you haven't met the 5 year holding period requirement, you will be subject to taxes, but no penalties. If you have met the 5 year holding period requirement, you will be subject to neither taxes or penalties.

Quick Tips: a beneficiary can be any person or entity the owner of an IRA or retirement account chooses. Be sure to talk to your advisor or the custodian that holds your retirement account to make sure you have beneficiaries in place. Although not technically Qualified, Section 403(b) plans have many of the same distribution characteristics as 401(k) plans, particularly when it comes to early distributions. You can review this on the IRS website at www.irs.gov.

How do I roll over a retirement plan?

Remember that while you are still working for the employer at which you have a retirement plan, that retirement plan can't be rolled over into another retirement plan such as a new 401k or an IRA. When as a participant in a qualified plan you leave an employer, you have a few options with what to do with your plan balance. You can:

1. Receive a distribution and use for current consumption, paying all taxes and penalties
2. Leave funds in the former employer's plan until retirement
3. Roll over the retirement plan balance to a new employer's plan if accepted
4. Roll over the balance to an IRA

Rolling over the balance of a former employer's retirement plan into an IRA is an extremely popular option. An IRA provides you with direct ownership of the assets, the ability to lower investment fees and access to more investment options. You can continue to defer taxation by rolling all or a portion of distributions from a former employer's retirement plan into an IRA or another qualified plan within 60 days. Once deposited into an IRA or Qualified plan, funds are not subject to income tax until they are withdrawn. If funds are directly transferred to an IRA or Qualified plan as part of an eligible rollover, no withholding tax applies. If a distribution rollover from a qualified plan is made directly to you, it will be subject to a 20% withholding tax. If you as the participant execute a rollover within 60 days of receiving the distribution from a Qualified plan, and follow all applicable IRS rules, the distribution will continue to grow tax-deferred in the new account.

Direct transfers and rollovers are allowed among Qualified plans, Section 403(b) plans, IRAs and some Section 457 plans as shown below.

Type of Distribution	Rollover allowed to a
From a qualified plan	Qualified plan or IRA
Section 403(b) plan/TDA	Qualified plan or IRA
Section 457 plan (eligible plan)	Qualified plan or IRA
Surviving spouse beneficiary	Qualified plan or IRA
Pursuant to a QDRO	Qualified plan or IRA
SIMPLE IRA (after 2 years)	Qualified plan or IRA
Section 457 plan (non-governmental)	Qualified plan or IRA
After-tax contribution to an IRA	IRA only

Source: *Certified Financial Planner ® website, cfp.net.*

Generally, all distributions are eligible for a rollover aside from (i) a distribution that is one of a series of substantially equal periodic payments and (ii) Required Minimum Distributions (RMDs) that typically begin when the participant reaches age 70 ½.

Certain Qualified plans benefit from cash-out rules when Qualified plan balances are below certain levels. If you are a participant with non-forfeitable balances of $5,000 or less it may be involuntarily cashed out. If the value of such a plan is greater than $1,000, but less than $5,000 the employer must provide you with a rollover option.

How do I convert an existing IRA to a Roth IRA (Roth Conversion)?

You can convert some or all of your existing balance in a traditional IRA to a Roth IRA regardless of your income level or participation in other retirement accounts. This is called a "Roth Conversion". When you move pre-tax funds from a traditional IRA to a Roth IRA, you pay income tax on these converted funds. This makes sense because if you had put the money in a Roth originally, all taxes would have been due upon contribution.

The Tax Code requires all deductible (pre-tax) and non-deductible (post-tax) traditional IRA funds be aggregated together and treated as a single IRA when making any sort of distribution or converting to a Roth IRA. This prevents you from being able to only distribute or convert non-taxable funds while leaving taxable funds in the traditional IRA. A Roth conversion is attractive if you expect your future tax rate to be higher than your current rate. The tax-free withdrawals available from your Roth IRA can be especially helpful in managing your taxes during retirement.

Quick Tip: you can estimate the tax you'll incur through a Roth conversion online, Fidelity offers a particularly good calculator.

What is a Required Minimum Distribution (RMD)?

If you participate in Qualified plans, Section 403(b) plans, or an IRA you are required by the Tax Code to take distributions from your plan once you reach a certain age. The first distribution must be made by April 1st of the year after the year you attain age 70 ½. In subsequent years, the distribution must be made by December 31st. If you delay the first distribution until April 1st following the year you reach age 70 ½, there will be two distributions in that calendar year, increasing the taxable income you as an account owner must recognize.

If you participate in a Qualified plan or Section 403(b) plan (but not an IRA) you can defer the required beginning date until April 1st following the year of retirement if you continue to work after reaching age 70 ½. This option to delay an RMD is not available if you are a 5% owner of the business sponsoring the retirement plan and is only available as part of your current employer's plan. If you do not take an RMD when required, you will incur a 50% excise tax on any shortfall. The RMD amount is determined each year by dividing the account balance at the close of business on December 31st of the previous year by the distribution period in the Uniform Distribution Table provided by the IRS. A participant must then replicate this calculation in each subsequent year to determine their RMD. The one exception to this calculation is if the participant's spouse is their designated beneficiary and the spouse is more than 10 years younger than the participant. In this case, a different Uniform Life Table must be used.

Quick Tip: the Uniform Distribution Table along with helpful worksheets used to calculate RMDs can be found directly on the IRS website irs.com.

How are distributions made from my retirement plan after death?

All Qualified plans (refer back to the exhibit at the beginning of this chapter if you can't remember which plans are Qualified) must offer two forms of survivorship benefits for a participant's spouse. The first is a Qualified Pre-retirement Survivor Annuity (QPSA) which must be offered by a defined benefit plan if a married participant with a vested benefit dies before he or she begins receiving benefits. This survivor annuity is called a qualified pre-retirement survivor annuity (QPSA). The second form of survivorship benefit, a Qualified Joint and Survivor Annuity (QJSA) is a type of contract that can be entered into in order to provide retirement benefits for two individuals. Typically, this is a type of annuity that is purchased by married couples. With a joint and survivor annuity, the annuity payments will be received for the duration of the lives of both people in the contract. If one of the spouses passes away, the other one will still be able to continue receiving annuity payments for the remainder of his or her life. This annuity will have smaller payments than an annuity for a single person. A waiver of either of these types of annuities requires irrevocable consent in writing by both participant and spouse witnessed by a notary or a plan official. A designated beneficiary must be determined as of September 30th following the year of a participant's death. The form of benefits is dependent on if the plan owner passes away before the date they must take RMDs (known as the Required Beginning Date) and whether the beneficiary is the participant's spouse.

Death before Required Beginning Date

If you are the surviving spouse and beneficiary of the plan, you have a few options. As the surviving spouse you can (i) elect to receive the entire account balance within five years (ii) roll the funds into an account in the original account owners name (an inherited IRA) and receive distributions over your own remaining single-life expectancy. Distributions must begin in the year in which the original account owner would have been 70 ½ or (iii) roll the funds into your own IRA and defer the funds until you turn 70 ½. This option will spread distributions over a longer period of time.

If as the beneficiary you are someone other than the surviving spouse (non-spouse beneficiary) you have two options (i) elect to receive the entire account balance within five years (ii) roll the funds into an account in the original account owners name (an inherited IRA) and receive distributions over your remaining single-life expectancy. In each subsequent year, the calculation is replicated with the life expectancy reduced by one. As a non-spouse beneficiary, you do not have the option to roll the funds into your own IRA.

Death after Required Beginning Date

If you are the surviving spouse and the beneficiary of the plan you can (i) roll the funds into an account in the original account owners name (an inherited IRA) and receive distributions over your own remaining single-life expectancy (recalculated each year). Your distributions must begin in the year following the account owner's death or you can (ii) roll the funds into your own IRA and defer distribution of the funds until you turn 70 ½. Note that the five-year distribution rule is not an option.

If as the beneficiary you are someone other than the surviving spouse (non-spouse beneficiary) you can roll the funds into an account in the original account owners name (an inherited IRA) and receive distributions over your own remaining single-life expectancy. In each subsequent year, the calculation is replicated with the life expectancy reduced by one. As a non-spouse beneficiary, you still do not have the option to roll the funds into your own IRA, but can take the distribution as a lump sum.

Can I access a loan through my retirement plan?

Another way in which you can potentially access funds through a retirement plan is a loan. Any type of Qualified plan or Section 403(b) plan may permit loans (but doesn't have to), however usually only Section 401(k) and Section 403(b) plans have loan provisions. IRAs do not permit loans. All loans must be repaid within five years aside from loans used to acquire a principal residence. If the loan is for a principal residence, it must be paid back in a "reasonable" timeframe which usually corresponds to the length of a mortgage loan (15 years, 30 years etc.).

Plan loans must be made available to all employees and not just Highly Compensated Employees (HCEs). Generally, loans are limited to one-half the present value of the participant's non-forfeitable accrued benefit or vested account balance and can't exceed $50,000. When a participant's vested account is less than $20,000 exceptions to the 50% limit may be made. When account balances are less than $20,000 up to $10,000 is available for a loan. When account balances are $10,000 or less, the vested account balance is available for a loan. The loans must be amortized on a level basis with payments made by participant-borrower at least quarterly.

The maximum loan amount may be further reduced by any loan balance you have in the one-year period preceding the loan. This keeps you from using the loan program as a type of revolver. Loans must be repaid in full upon separation from service. If the loan is not repaid in full, the outstanding balance at the time of separation is treated as a taxable distribution and is possibly subject to the 10% early distribution penalty.

What is a Qualified Domestic Relations Order (QDRO)?

In general, the benefits of a Qualified plan can't be assigned by the current owner/participant. This protects your retirement funds from creditors. A QDRO is an exception to this rule.

A QDRO is a decree, order or property settlement under a state law relating to child support, alimony, or marital property rights that assigns all or part of an owner/participant's benefits to an alternate payee. This alternate payee can include a spouse, former spouse, child or other dependent. QDRO's specify the time at which the alternate payee will receive the plan benefit, but can't change the form of payment to one that is not initially in the retirement plan. The subsequent spouse of an alternate payee (the former spouse's new spouse) may not receive the survivor benefit rights from the plan.

An alternate payee who is a former spouse of a plan participant and who receives a QDRO distribution may roll over the distribution into another retirement plan in the same manner as if he or she were the participant. Distributions from a Qualified plan made to an alternate payee pursuant to a QDRO will be subject to income tax, but will not be subject to the 10% early withdrawal penalty.

Further Resources

- **www.blackrock.com/iRetire** – Blackrock's retirement-centered portion of the website that can help you with retirement planning. You will have to create a username and password, but the free retirement calculator tool is worth it. The tool provides not only suggested savings to reach your goals, but does a good job of explaining the types of investments that can help you get there.

- **www.mymoney.gov** – U.S. government's website on personal finance. Go to "Life Events" and select the Retirement/Retirement Planning section. The section provides numerous articles, tools and resources on the different aspects of retirement.

- **www.finra.org/investors/401k-rollovers** – Financial Industry Regulatory Authority (FINRA) website that provides extensive detail on the how and why of rolling over a retirement plan into an Individual Retirement Account (IRA). Provides additional links on making this rollover decision as well.

- **www.kiplinger.com** – the Kiplinger personal finance website has a "Retirement" section that is a great source for new updates and articles that will impact your retirement (changes to contribution limits, taxes etc.).

- **www.irs.com** – official IRS website. Information is very dry, but useful. Simply enter the retirement plan or topic you are seeking information on in the keyword search. There are a number of very good "white paper" style publications.

Books:

Taking the Mystery Out of Retirement Planning; U.S. Department of Labor

Provided by the U.S. Department of Labor. Light on content, but a good start on planning for retirement. Free download at http://www.dol.gov/ebsa/publications/nearretirement.html or call toll free 866-444-3272 to order copies.

Tuttle, John C. *IRAs, 401(k)s & Other Retirement Plans: Taking Your Money Out.* Nolo. 2017.

In depth guide to help you understand your retirement plan and how to take money out of it. Makes sense of the complex tax rules governing when you can take money out of your plan and how much. Will advise you on avoiding the penalties and taxes that can occur if you do not follow retirement plan rules and regulations. Make sure to get the most updated version of the text.

Chapter 6: Social Security

✓ Sign up for a MySocialSecurity account at the Social Security website www.ssa.gov to gain access to all your Social Security data as well as tools to estimate your benefits.

✓ Review the role Social Security will play in your retirement. What percentage of annual cash flows will Social Security provide in comparison to other assets?

✓ Analyze the different variables that will impact your Social Security such as when you file for benefits and your spouse's benefit situation.

✓ Understand how to file for your Social Security benefits when the time comes to do so. You will need specific documents and can file either online, over the phone or in person.

Most of us don't realize it, but Social Security is actually a general term to describe a series of federal programs that fund retirement, survivor, dependent and disability benefits. Your Social Security benefit payments are not related to need, but instead to your past earnings and the taxes you paid on these earnings. These taxes you paid helped fund Social Security programs.

Social Security uses your top 35 earning years as the basis in calculating the benefit (known as your primary insurance amount) you will receive once you reach your Full Retirement Age (FRA). Your benefits will rise annually based on a cost-of-living adjustment and you are not able to receive more than one Social Security benefit at any time.

It is important to keep in mind, particularly when constructing a cash flow budget, that Social Security benefits are intended to supplement a certain percentage of you or a loved one's income, but not replace this income in its entirety.

What are the different types of Social Security benefits?

There are three main types of Social Security benefits; retirement benefits, survivor benefits and disability benefits. At some point, you might be eligible to receive any of the three types of benefits. In addition, a number of dependents such as your spouse, children and even parents can be eligible for these benefits. The value of the Social Security benefits you receive is dependent not only on your past earnings, but the number of Social Security work credits you have and the age at which you file for your Social Security benefits.

Retirement benefits are what most of us think of when we think about Social Security benefits. Full retirement benefits are received at Full Retirement Age (FRA). FRA is the age at which you may first become entitled to full or unreduced retirement benefits. FRA can range from age 65 to age 67 depending on your date of birth. Retirement benefits provide lifetime income based on your average earnings during your working years. Those eligible to receive retirement benefits include:

- Retired worker (age 62 or older)
- Spouse of retired worker (age 62 or older) note that current spouse has to wait for retired worker to file for benefits
- Divorced spouse (married 10 years to covered worker) who is 62 or older regardless of workers actual retirement
- Unmarried children under age 18, age 19 if still in high school or any age if child is disabled before age 22
- Caretaker spouse of any age with a dependent child under age 16 or a child disabled before age

Survivors benefits were created to care for dependents of the workers who die before (or after) reaching their FRA. Those eligible to receive survivor benefits include:

- Surviving spouse of retired worker (age 60 or older)
- Divorced spouse (married 10 years to covered worker)
- Unmarried children under age 18, age 19 if still in high school or any age if child is disabled before age 22
- Caretaker spouse of any age with a dependent child under age 16 or a child disabled before age 22
- Disabled widow(er) (ages 50 – 60; fully insured only)
- Dependent parents of deceased worker (age 62 and over; fully insured only)

Disability benefits provide for a qualified worker who becomes totally and permanently disabled. You must meet Social Security's definition of disability (no gainful employment) with the disability expected to last 12 months or result in death. Those eligible to receive disability benefits include:

- Disabled worker
- Spouse of disabled worker
- Unmarried children under age 18, age 19 if still in high school or any age if child is disabled

How do I qualify for Social Security benefits?

When you work and pay social security taxes, you earn "credits" towards Social Security benefits. A credit is earned for each $1,300 of earnings on which Social Security taxes are paid. You can earn a maximum of 4 of these credits annually.

Retirement benefits require you to be fully insured which means you have 40 credits of coverage (roughly 10 years of Social Security covered employment) or one credit of coverage for each year over the age of 21. Fully insured for the purposes of survivor's benefits depends on the workers year of birth.

Currently insured applies only to a spouse or child claiming survivor benefits and refers to a situation in which a deceased person earned 6 credits in the 13 quarter period prior to their death.

Disability insurance requires you to be fully insured with at least 20 credits in the last 40 quarters. It is possible to be disability insured with less than 20 credits. If you are between the age of 24 and 30 you can qualify if you have coverage for half of the quarters since age 21 or if you are under age 24, you can qualify for disability benefits if you have received 6 credits during the last 12 quarters.

With questions on your benefits, contact either a trusted advisor or the Social Security Administration via their website at www.socialsecurity.gov or toll free at 1-800-772-1213. In addition, most cities have a local Social Security office you can visit in person. We recommend that if you have not done so already that you sign up for a "my Social Security" account to access your current Social Security data.

How does filing age impact my Social Security benefits?

Your Full Retirement Age (FRA) depends on the year of your birth. Your FRA is the age at which you will receive your full amount of Social Security benefits. This full amount of benefits is referred to as your Primary Insurance Amount (PIA). Note that each year not represented in the exhibit below equates to 2 months in additional FRA.

Year	Full Retirement Age
1937 and earlier	65
1943 - 1945	66
1960 and later	67

If you elect to receive benefits prior to your FRA your benefits will be reduced. If you delay the receipt of your Social Security benefits the value of your annual benefits will rise for each year you delay through age 70. The increase in your annual benefits is 8% if you were born in 1943 or later and slightly less than 8% if you were born prior to 1943.

The earliest you as a worker can receive retirement benefits is age 62. If you elect to receive benefits prior to your FRA, the maximum reduction in retirement benefits is 30% if your FRA is 67 and 20% if your FRA is 65. This means if you elect to file for benefits earlier than your FRA there will be a reduction in your benefits as follows:

- 5/9 of 1% per month prior to your FRA up to 36 months
- 5/12 of 1% per month prior to your FRA beyond 36 months

The exhibit below shows the impact on benefits of an early or delayed benefit claim assuming an FRA of 66.

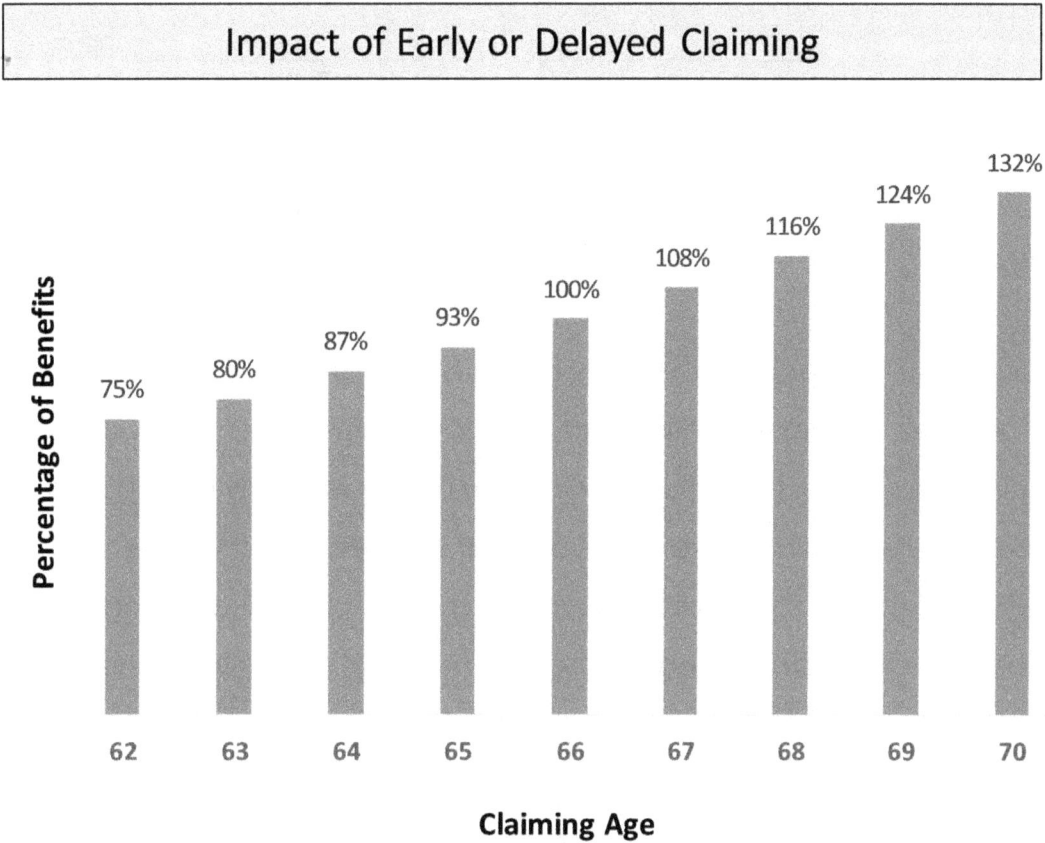

Impact of Early or Delayed Claiming

Claiming Age	Percentage of Benefits
62	75%
63	80%
64	87%
65	93%
66	100%
67	108%
68	116%
69	124%
70	132%

If you are a current or ex-spouse (an ex-spouse must have been married for 10 years and not remarry prior to age 60) you may be eligible for Social Security spousal benefits. When you file for Social Security retirement benefits, you are automatically entitled to receive a benefit based on your own earnings or a spousal benefit. Social Security calculates and pays you the higher benefit. You are not eligible to receive a spousal benefit until your spouse files for their own benefits. There are different rules if you are an ex-spouse. Even if your ex-spouse has not filed for their own benefits, you can receive spousal benefits if your ex-spouse is age 62 or older.

If you file for dependent benefits based on your spouse's earnings there will be a reduction in benefits as per the exhibit below.

Age	% of Full Benefit
62	35.0%
63	37.5%
64	41.7%
65	45.8%
FRA	50.0%

If your spouse files for Social Security benefits early and you take a spousal benefit early you will be significantly reducing your current benefits and significantly reducing the survivor benefits for which you may eventually be eligible. A surviving spouse at age 60 will receive 71.5% of what the deceased worker's full retirement benefits will be. Each year a surviving spouse delays claiming benefits, the percentage of the deceased spouse's benefits will rise until reaching 100% at the surviving spouses FRA. Married couples can receive much more in Social Security payments over the course of a lifetime by coordinating their benefit collections. This is especially important since the passage of the new Social Security laws in November 2015 which ended "restricted applications" and "file and suspend", two popular methods of maximizing spousal Social Security benefits.

Quick Tip: You can use the Social Security Administration website at www.socialsecurity.gov to calculate your spousal benefits and make sure you are maximizing payments.

When should I file for Social Security Benefits?

There is no simple answer to the best time to claim social security. If you claim benefits early, you will collect benefits for a longer period of time, but the permanent reduction in monthly benefits resulting from an early filing means that if you live past a certain age, you will wind up with less benefits over the course of your lifetime.

For our example, lets assume a beneficiary's full payment at FRA is $1,000 per month. If the beneficiary files at age 62 they will receive $750 per month and if they delay filing until age 70 they will receive $1,320 per month.

- When filing at age 62, $750 will be received every month for 48 months until the beneficiary's FRA of 66. This results in a $36,000 inflow. Filing for benefits at age 66 results in $250 of additional inflow each month ($1,000 vs. $750). At $250 per month it will take 144 months ($36,000/$250) or roughly 12 years to break-even. Therefore, the break-even age when choosing to file for benefits at either age 66 or age 62 is 78 years old. This means if you live past age 78 your decision to delay filing until age 66 will have paid off.

We went over the variance in your benefit values depending on when you file for Social Security benefits at length, but there are several other factors you should take into account when deciding on the timing of a Social Security benefit filing.

- Are you still working? There can be a reduction in your Social Security benefits if your income exceeds certain limits as we discuss in this chapter.
- Do you have any sense of your life expectancy (family health history)? It may not be worth delaying the receipt of your benefits if there is any indication that you will not live past the break-even age.

- Are you married, and do you have dependents? If your spouse or dependents file for Social Security benefits based on your earnings history, the benefits they receive may factor into a decision on when you file for benefits yourself.

- Do you need the cash flow? This one may seem obvious, but these are your benefits and you earned them. There is no use delaying the receipt of Social Security benefits if you are in a situation where you definitely need to boost your current cash flows.

Quick Tip: discuss the decision of when to take Social Security with your family and friends. Consult an advisor and contact the Social Security Administration (www.ssa.gov, 1-800-772-1213) for clarification. The ins and outs of Social Security can be confusing, but don't stop asking questions until you are comfortable with the answers you have and your Social Security decision.

Can my Social Security benefits be reduced?

An earnings test applies to your Social Security benefits only if you have not reached Full Retirement Age (FRA). This earnings test applies only to your "earned income". Earned income does not include:

- Interest on savings and investments
- Capital gains
- IRA or 401(k) withdrawals
- Insurance cash-ins
- Rent or royalties
- Private pensions

There are a number of situations in which Social Security benefits may be reduced. Until you reach your FRA, the Social Security administration will deduct $1 from your Social Security benefits for every $2 you receive over the 2018 earned income limit of $16,920 ($1,410 / month). If you are already receiving retirement benefits, a special higher earnings limit applies in the 12 months leading up to your FRA. You may earn up to $44,880 in the period before the month you reach FRA. For every $3 above this value, $1 will be deducted from your Social Security benefits.

Another special rule applies if you claim retirement benefits prior to FRA. During the first year you claim your Social Security benefits, you can get a full Social Security benefit payment for any one month in which your earnings are less than the maximum allowed by Social Security, ($1,410/month) regardless of annual earnings.

Self-employed retirees who work more than 45 hours in a month are not considered retired. If you are a self-employed retiree that works between 15 and

45 hours, whether you are considered retired is dependent upon the skill your job requires.

A person receiving disability benefits can earn just over $1,000/month before limiting the benefits they receive. The maximum disability benefits a worker and their family can receive is 85% of the workers prior earnings or 150% of what the workers individual benefit is.

A government pension offset will apply to your Social Security benefits if you previously received a pension under the Civil Service Retirement System that paid no Social Security taxes. If this is the case, your Social Security benefits will be reduced dollar for dollar by 2/3rds of the value of your civil service pension.

Can my Social Security benefits be taxed?

Once you reach Full Retirement Age (FRA) your Social Security benefits will not be reduced based on your earnings, but they can be taxed if your provisional income exceeds certain levels. Your provisional income is defined as your Modified Adjusted Gross Income (MAGI) plus one half of your Social Security benefits. The thresholds for provisional income are shown below.

- Up to 50% of your Social Security benefits will be taxed if your provisional income exceeds:
  - $34,000 if you are married taxpayers filing jointly
  - $0 if you are married taxpayers filing separately
  - $25,000 for all other filers

- Up to 85% of your Social Security benefits will be taxed if your provisional income exceeds:
  - $44,000 if you are married taxpayers filing jointly
  - $0 if you are married taxpayers filing separately
  - $32,000 for all other filers

How do I apply for benefits and navigate the Social Security website?

Once you have made the decision of when to begin receiving benefits, applying for these benefits is usually fairly simple. The application process for retirement, dependent and survivor benefits all involve the same basic documents and procedures. When you first apply for Social Security benefits do not expect to be told exactly what your benefits will be. It will take 6 – 8 weeks to have the national Social Security office process your claim. The best thing you can do wherever you are in the process is to set up a "my Social Security" account at www.ssa.gov/myaccount/ if you have not done so already. This will allow you to access and familiarize yourself with your own Social Security information. If you are having any issues with setting up your account you can call Social Security at 1-800-772-1213. In addition, at any point in the process, you can always visit your local Social Security office in person.

- You should start to examine your most recent Social Security statement six months before you might claim Social Security benefits. Your Social Security statement contains estimates of the value of your benefits if you choose to file at various ages.

- File your claim three months prior to when you would like to receive your Social Security benefits to give the Social Security administration time to process your claim.

- When applying for retirement benefits, you will need some or all of the following data and documents:
  - Your Social Security Number
  - Your birth certificate or any other evidence of your date of birth
  - Most recent W-2 or federal self-employment tax return
  - For dependents benefits you will need a marriage certificate for a spouse and a birth certificate for children

- For survivors benefits you will need some additional data and documents:
  - Social Security Number and death certificate of the deceased person
  - Divorce papers if applying as a divorced spouse
  - If your spouse died within the past two years, the deceased spouse's most recent W-2

If for any reason you need to withdrawal a benefits application you can do so within 12 months, provided you repay all benefits you have received up to that point. When applying for Disability claims it is a bit more complex and the Social Security Administration typically requires 2 – 6 months to process the claim. Documentation from the institutions that have diagnosed your medical conditions is required.

Further Resources

• **www.socialsecurity.gov** – this is the official Social Security website. You can sign up for a "mySocialSecurity" account to see your current benefits. In addition when it comes time to sign up for benefits you can do so directly on the website. There is good background information in the "Apply for Retirement" section. Once entering this section, there is an extremely useful "Benefits Calculator" option that allows you to estimate your future Social Security benefits.

• **www.nasi.org** – website is nonprofit, nonpartisan organization with the mission of raising the public understanding of social insurance. Provides very informative summary information and white papers on social security.

• **www.aarp.org** – under the "Work and Retirement" section there is a specific Social Security option with some great resources including a Social Security calculator.

• **www.kiplinger.com** – you have to register for the Kiplinger website, but it's a very good resource for retirement and Social Security, particularly the day-to-day articles.

• **www.nolo.com** – more legal-based website with a very informative section on Social Security and retirement under the "Get Informed" option.

Books:

Kotlikoff, Laurence J. *Get Whats Yours: The Secrets to Maxing out Your Social Security*. Simon & Schuster. 2017.
Good, succinct and straight-forward summary information on Social Security as well as useful tips on the best methods and strategies in claiming your Social Security.

Matthews, Joseph. *Social Security, Medicare & Government Pensions: Get the Most Out of Your Retirement & Medical Benefits.* **Nolo. 2017.**

A more legal-centric, reference-style book, that helps you figure out how to get retirement, disability, dependent and survivors benefits along with deciding when its best to claim. Make sure you get the most up-to-date version of this text.

Chapter 7: Your Medicare

✓ Familiarize yourself with the four different parts of Medicare. Medicare Part A (hospital bills), Part B (doctor's expenses), Part C (Medicare Advantage plans) and Part D (drug costs).

✓ Figure out if a separate Medigap program should be used to supplement the gaps in the coverage of Medicare Part A and Part B.

✓ Understand how you qualify for Medicare and how you apply for your benefits at www.medicare.gov.

✓ If you stop work before you qualify for Medicare at age 65, look into the use and rules of the Consolidated Omnibus Budget Reconciliation Act (COBRA).

For more than 40 years, the federal Medicare program has helped citizens 65 and older as well as certain disabled citizens cover the cost of hospitalization and other medical care. Medicare Part A covers hospital costs, while Medicare Part B pays some doctors expenses as well as outpatient medical care. Medicare Part C refers to Medicare Advantage Plans which offer identical services to both Medicare Part A and Medicare Part B as well as some extended coverage. Medicare Part D pays certain prescription drug costs.

Medicare is operated by the Department of Health and Human Services in conjunction with the Social Security Administration. Medicare's day-to-day operations, however utilize private insurance companies that contract with the federal government.

Despite an extensive reach, Medicare pays only a portion of medical services and does not cover many types of medical services all together. This causes consumers to purchase either Medigap insurance policies or a Medicare Advantage Plan to supplement shortfalls in traditional Medicare Part A and Part

B. For those low-income and disabled Americans that qualify, Medicaid can work either alongside Medicare or instead of Medicare to cover a large portion of medical needs and costs.

Medicare can be a complicated topic. It is important to utilize some key resources when trying to understand your Medicare benefits, particularly when dealing with your payments or filing an appeal. Do not hesitate to contact Medicare directly at www.medicare.gov or toll free at 800 – MEDICARE. In addition, your state will provide you with extensive assistance through the State Health Insurance Assistance Program (SHIP) which you can access at www.shiptacenter.org.

What is Medicare and what should I do prior to applying for Medicare?

Through traditional Medicare older Americans and certain disabled citizens can receive care from a doctor, hospital, clinic or other provider that accepts Medicare patients. Medicare operates in 4 separate parts. Medicare Part A covers hospital costs, while Medicare Part B pays some doctors expenses as well as outpatient medical care. Medicare Part C refers to a Medicare Advantage Plan which offers the same coverage as Medicare Part A and Medicare Part B as well as some extended coverage. Medicare Part D pays certain prescription drug costs.

Medicare pays your provider a fee for each service. For services Medicare does not fully pay for, you can:

- Pay out-of-pocket.
- Purchase a private supplemental insurance policy known as a Medigap insurance policy.
- For uncovered drug expenses purchase a Medicare Part D prescription drug plan as part of a separate insurance plan.
- If you qualify based on certain income thresholds, apply for low-income Medicaid coverage.

If you will turn 65 in the near future and plan on applying for Medicare, there are a few things you will want to address prior to applying.

- Find out if your current health insurance will continue when you hit age 65 and if your current health coverage will continue how it will work in conjunction with Medicare.
- Speak to your current doctor(s) and other service providers to inquire if they accept Medicare and the nature of their relationship with Medicare (any issues in the past)?

- Find out which Medigap insurance policies are available in your geographic region to help supplement Medicare Part A and Medicare Part B.

- Figure out what Medicare Part C Plans (Medicare Advantage Plans) are available in your geographic region to supplement/replace Medicare Part A and Medicare Part B.

- Get up to speed on the Medicare Part D plans available in your state. Make sure to inquire about the specific drugs you need.

- If you believe you may qualify, inquire about Medicaid, or other state assistance that can help supplement your Medicare costs.

Quick Tip: You can find extensive information on Medigap policies and Medicare Advantage Plans at www.medicare.gov.

How do I qualify and apply for Medicare?

Most people age 65 and older are automatically eligible for Medicare Part A hospital insurance. Medicare Part A is a social benefit, based on Medicare taxes you have paid during your working years. You should qualify for Medicare Part A if you have worked at least 10 years (40 quarters) and paid Medicare taxes during that time. The payroll tax percentage used to fund Medicare is 2.9% annually. This percentage applies only to your earned income and typically you pay 1.45% and your employer pays 1.45%. If you do not qualify for Medicare Part A you can enroll and pay a monthly premium based on your number of Social Security work credits. If you receive Social Security disability benefits for two years you will automatically be enrolled in Medicare Part A. If you will soon be 65, but are not receiving Social Security benefits, you can apply during a seven month initial enrollment period that includes the three months prior to your 65th birthday and the four months after your 65th birthday. If you do not enroll during this initial seven month period, you must enroll during a general enrollment period from January 1st to March 31st and your coverage will begin on July 1st of the year you enroll. If you lose your employer-sponsored group hospital insurance, you will be allowed to enroll during the eight month period after you lose this insurance.

Anyone who is eligible for free Medicare Part A is eligible for Medicare Part B simply by enrolling and paying a monthly premium. If you are not eligible for Medicare Part A you can still qualify for Medicare Part B if you are 65 or older and a U.S. citizen or permanent resident. You can enroll in Medicare Part B during an initial 7 month period that spans the 3 months prior to when you turn 65 and the 4 months after your 65th birthday. If you do not enroll in Medicare Part B during this initial 7 month period, you will have to enroll during a general enrollment period from January 1st through March 31st. Coverage in this scenario will begin on July 1st of the year in which you enrolled during the general enrollment period. The standard Part B Medicare monthly premium is $134 in 2018, but can be more depending on your income. For each year you delay enrolling in Medicare Part B, your premium may rise. If you delay enrolling in Medicare Part B because you are covered by an employer plan, you may enroll during a special enrollment period that lasts eight months after your employer coverage ends without penalty.

When signing up for Medicare Part D, you will contact the private insurance company that administers the Medicare Part D Plan directly. Each Medicare Part D Plan will have different forms, procedures and timing. If you are going to enroll in a Medicare Part D Plan it is a good idea to do so a few months before you want your coverage to begin because your drug expenses will not be covered while your application is pending. In addition, there is a 1% premium increase for each month you delay your Medicare Part D enrollment.

Quick Tip: you can apply for Medicare Part A or Medicare Part B on the Social Security website www.socialsecurity.gov or call the Social Security administration at 1-800-772-1213.

What is Medicare Part A and what does it cover?

Medicare Part A covers hospital inpatient costs as well as certain other hospital-related medical services. Qualifying for Medicare Part A is not tied to individual need, but instead is an entitlement based on Social Security taxes you paid over the course of your lifetime. Most people are automatically eligible for Medicare Part A at age 65 if they have worked at least 10 years (40 quarters) and paid Medicare tax during that time.

In terms of hospital expenses, Medicare Part A requires you to pay an initial deductible of $1,316. After this deductible, Medicare Part A covers all costs for the first 60 days of a hospital stay. For days 60 – 90 of a hospital stay, Medicare Part A covers all costs aside from a daily coinsurance amount of $329 per day. Past 90 days, there are 60 reserve days of coverage that require a coinsurance amount of $658 per day. Although there are out-of-pocket expenses needed to cover premiums and deductibles, the most burdensome Medicare Part A expenses tend to be the hospital coinsurance payments that begin on day 60 of your stay. Many consumers purchase Medigap insurance policies, or opt for a Medicare Advantage Plan to help make sure these hospital coinsurance payments are covered.

Medicare Part A will cover a number of other medical expenses aside from your hospital bills. Some of the major non-hospital expenses covered by Medicare Part A include:

- The cost of your first 100 days of inpatient treatment in a skilled nursing facility. To qualify for skilled nursing facility care you must have previously had a hospital stay of at least three days. You are fully covered for the first 20 days of your 100-day facility stay. For the next 80 days you will be responsible for co-payments of $167.50 per day.

- Certain costs of care provided by a home health agency. There is no limit on the number of home healthcare days covered by Medicare Part A. A doctor must certify that you are home-bound in order to receive these services.
- A total of 190 days in a specialty psychiatric hospital.
- Medicare Part A can cover nearly the full cost of hospice care.

Not included as part of the expenses covered by Medicare Part A is custodial care, which typically involves assistance with the tasks of daily living. Tasks of daily living include eating, dressing, bathing and moving around. This assistance most often occurs in a nursing home, but can occur in your home as well. This custodial care can last for months or even years and is different than the care that is covered by Medicare provided in a skilled nursing facility. The skilled nursing care covered by Medicare most often follows serious illness, injury or surgery. The covered care will require high levels of specialization care and will last for a matter of days or weeks. Custodial care costs are not covered by Medicare or Medigap insurance policies. If you are worried about custodial care costs examine funding options including Long-term Care Insurance discussed later in this book.

What is Medicare Part B and what does it cover?

Medicare Part B is medical insurance that is used to help pay doctor bills or medical expenses when you are not in a hospital. If you are age 65 or older and either a U.S. citizen or resident for 5 years you are eligible to apply for Medicare Part B regardless of if you are enrolled in Medicare Part A. The base monthly premium for Medicare Part B is $134 in 2018, but this premium may be higher if your income exceeds certain thresholds. If you receive monthly Social Security benefits, you can have this Part B premium deducted directly from your Social Security benefits.

Below are a number of services for which Medicare Part B provides full or partial coverage. In general, the key to the coverage of these treatments is their medical necessity and/or prescription by a medical professional. If at any time you have coverage questions be sure to call 800-MEDICARE or contact your State Health Insurance Assistance Program (SHIP).

- Medically necessary doctor's services, including surgery
- Outpatient services provided by a hospital
- Necessary transportation by ambulance
- Medical equipment and supplies recommended by a doctor
- Drugs administered to you at a hospital or doctor's office (not at home)
- Skilled home health care costs not covered by Medicare Part A
- Laboratory services
- Preventative care screenings
- Flu and pneumonia vaccines
- When prescribed by a hospital, counseling by a social worker or psychologist
- Some costs of outpatient physical and speech therapy
- Some costs of a Medicare-certified chiropractor
- Certain types of Alzheimer-related treatments Quick

It is important to understand that Medicare Part B is intended to pay for only some of the services provided by doctors, clinics and laboratories. When all your expenses are added up, Medicare Part B will only pay a portion of your expenses for the following reasons (i) Medicare Part B doesn't cover a number of medical expenses including routine physical exams, glasses, hearing aids, dentures etc. and (ii) Medicare Part B pays only "approved charges" and you typically cover a 20% co-payment. This leads some consumers to purchase either Medigap insurance policies or Medicare Advantage Plans to help cover expenses not paid for by Medicare Part B. The uncovered Part B medical expenses include:

- The annual deductible, which is $183 in 2018.
- If your doctor accepts Medicare assignment, you will be responsible for 20% of total costs (Medicare Part B covers the other 80%).
- If your doctor does not accept Medicare assignment, you will be responsible for 20% of total costs plus up to 15% more of the Medicare approved amount.
- A key gap in Medicare Part B coverage is that although some home healthcare is covered, the care is always short-term and limited to a period of recovery from acute injury or illness. The kind of long-term care that many older people need either at home or in a facility, due to frailty or inability to perform activities of daily life (most likely provided in a nursing home facility) is not covered. If this coverage is desired, you should explore Long-Term Care Insurance or examine the possibility of funding these costs yourself.

Quick Tip: your Part B premiums may rise above the $134 base if your earned income hits certain levels as detailed on www.medicare.gov.

What is Medicare Part C and what does it cover?

If you qualify for or are already enrolled in Medicare Part A and Medicare Part B, you can choose to enroll in Medicare Part C, which is generally referred to as Medicare Advantage. Medicare Advantage works a bit differently than the other parts of Medicare and is available based on the geographic region in which you live. Medicare Advantage Plans are offered by private insurance companies and provide the exact same coverage as Medicare Part A and Medicare Part B (this coverage is required by Federal law). In addition, Medicare Advantage fills in some of the gaps left by Medicare Part A and Medicare Part B through extended coverage. Some Medicare Advantage Plans also offer Medicare Part D drug coverage. If you purchase a Medicare Advantage Plan you will still remain enrolled in Medicare Part A and Medicare Part B and will continue to pay Medicare Part B premiums. Medicare Advantage Plans are offered in two forms:

(i) Managed Care Plan – in return for medical coverage you will pay a low (or no) monthly premium and small co-payments. Under Managed Care Plans your access to doctors and other providers is limited. Managed Care Plans are generally offered through a Health Maintenance Organization (HMO) under which you will have a primary care physician that must refer you to other medical service providers or specialists. If you receive care outside of the HMO's network of service providers you will generally be responsible for the full cost of service. Many times HMO's will offer a point-of-service option allowing you to visit out-of-network specialists without a referral. This option will require a higher premium and co-payment.

(ii) Fee-for-service Plan – in a Fee-for-service Plan, a specific amount is paid for your treatments and the service provider must accept the payment terms of the Medicare Advantage Plan. If the payment terms are not accepted you will end up paying elevated fees. This means you should make sure your provider accepts the Medicare assigned fees.

If you apply for a Medicare Advantage Plan three months before you turn age 65 or within four months after your 65th birthday you will have an unqualified right to join the Medicare Advantage plan that operates in in your county without medical screening. Every Medicare Advantage Plan must have an "open enrollment" period for one month of the year. If you do not enroll during this initial period, you will then have to enroll during the Annual Election Period that runs from October 15th through December 7th every year. If you enroll during this annual election period, your coverage will start January 1st of the following year. If you are dropped from a Medicare Advantage Plan you will be notified by October 1st. You will then have the opportunity to join another Medicare Advantage Plan or enroll in Medicare Part A and Medicare Part B with a Medigap policy without medical screening. To leave a Medicare Advantage Plan you must give 30 days notice between January 1st and February 14th of the year you would like to leave the plan.

Some of the gaps in Medicare Part A and Medicare Part B that Medicare Advantage Plans will cover are listed below. Be sure to check in with the particular plan you are considering to see exactly the extent of the coverage being offered.

- Short-term custodial care if you are not able to care for yourself, but skilled nursing care is not required. This type of care may be offered through a certified home health care agency or a certified nursing facility
- The 20% payment required under Medicare Part B when purchasing qualified durable medical equipment
- More chiropractic care than provided under Medicare
- Medical coverage during travel abroad
- Contributions towards eye exams and glasses
- Hearing exams and discounts on hearing aids
- Discounts on dental work

When examining a Medicare Advantage Plan make sure to review the Summary of Benefits document. This document will lay out the Medicare Advantage Plan's coverage, costs and procedures. In addition, on the medicare.gov website there is information on patient satisfaction ratings and statistics for Medicare Advantage Plans. Between the information on medicare.gov and the Summary of Benefits you should be able to get sufficient data on:

- Rejected referrals to a specialist
- Early discharges of a hospital inpatient
- Dropped coverage history for your geographic region
- Dropped doctors and hospitals from the network
- Past increases in co-payments
- Switched drugs on the plan formulary

If you need to appeal a decision by a Medicare Advantage Plan, after receiving written explanation denying a claim, you must submit a handwritten request for reconsideration within 60 days. The Medicare Advantage Plan must respond to your reconsideration request within 30 days if it's a service you want provided in the future. If the request for reconsideration involves a payment you've already made, the Medicare Advantage Plan must respond within 60 days. If there is a negative response to your request for reconsideration, contacting an independent outside entity to make a decision on your appeal is the next and final step.

What is Medicare Part D and what does it cover?

Medicare Part D provides some coverage for the cost of prescription drugs for those enrolled in Medicare. Medicare Part D is run by Medicare, but administered through private insurance companies as well as through Medicare Advantage Plans that include Medicare Part D drug benefits. When you enroll you pay a monthly premium to the insurance company. If you are entitled to Medicare Part A or enrolled in Medicare Part B, you may join a Medicare Part D prescription drug plan. The list of drugs covered by the Medicare Part D program is contained in each plan's formulary.

For Medicare Part D you will more than likely pay an initial deductible. Expenses are then covered 100% up to an initial cost threshold. Once your expenses reach that initial threshold, the plan pays roughly 75% while you pay 25% of your drug costs. There is then a "doughnut hole" when you have to cover all of your Medicare Part D expenses until your out-of-pocket costs reach a certain "upper threshold". Once your costs exceed this "upper threshold", Medicare Part D will pay 95% of all further costs and you will pay 5%.

Factors to consider when choosing a Medicare Part D Plan include the account premium, deductible and co-payment, availability of generic drugs as well as coverage of the "doughnut hole". Prior to choosing a Medicare Part D plan, contact the plan directly to get detail on the questions below.

- Which medications are in the formulary?
- What are the total monthly costs of drugs and the co-payments required?
- Is there first dollar coverage?
- Total of all costs (annual premium, yearly deductible, co-payments for drugs and out-of-pocket costs)?
- Access restrictions (drug substitutions, supply limits and pharmacy limitations)?

A Medicare Part D plan can often change drugs on their formulary or drop drugs in the plan all together. A Medicare Part D plan must provide you 60 days notice prior to changing its formulary. If a Medicare Part D plan drops a drug, its coverage of the drug must continue through the end of the year. You can switch Part D plans between October 15th and December 7th each year.

There are a number of Medicare Part D discount programs. You can find good information on such discount programs at www.medicare.gov which can direct you to state assistance programs or pharmaceutical discount programs. In addition, every state has programs offering free counseling and assistance on Medicare, Medicaid and other health insurance related questions. The two programs are (i) State Health Insurance Assistance Program (SHIP) and (ii) Health Insurance Counseling and Advocacy Program (HICAP).

Quick Tip: in addition to contacting the plan directly, you can reach out to your State Health Insurance Assistance Program (SHIP) https://www.shiptacenter.org/ with questions. To get a list of Medicare Part D Plans in your area you can access this information at www.medicare.gov under the "Medicare Plan Finder" section.

How do Medigap programs work to cover Medicare service gaps?

Medigap insurance policies can fill in some of the coverage holes left by Medicare Part A and Medicare Part B. You can purchase a Medigap policy only if you already have Medicare Part A and Medicare Part B and do not have a Medicare Part C Medicare Advantage Plan. The federal government regulates Medigap insurance policies to make sure they don't overlap with Medicare Plan A or Medicare Plan B. The federal government however, does not decide the pricing of Medigap policies, pricing is left to the private insurance companies that administer Medigap policies. Aside from price, you should look at the policy's history of premium increases and pre-existing illness exclusions when deciding on a Medigap policy. There are 10 different Medigap policy options (A, B,C,D,F,G,K,L,M and N), and all standard Medigap policies offer:

- Hospital coinsurance amounts under Medicare Part A
- 365 days of hospital coverage after Medicare Part A coverage ends
- Some or all of Medicare Part B coinsurance costs (20% of Medicare approved expenses that Medicare Part B does not pay)
- Some or all of the cost of blood transfusions
- Some or all out-of-pocket costs for hospice care

Medigap policy pricing can be impacted by inflation, geography and any discount you may receive. Your Medigap premiums can take a variety of forms including:

Community-rated (no-age-rated): premiums are the same for everyone, regardless of age.

Issue-age-rated (entry-age-rated): the premiums are based on your age when you first purchase the policy so the sooner you enroll, the less you will pay.

Attained-age-rated: premiums based on current age, so the premiums rise as you grow older.

Once you are both over 65 years old and have Medicare Part B, a six month open enrollment for Medigap insurance begins. This is the best time to enroll because you will not have to undergo medical screening or face coverage limitations. This applies if you leave a Medicare Advantage Plan within a year of age 65 as well. You must apply for a Medigap policy within 63 days of the date your Medicare Advantage coverage ends. If you did not enroll in Medicare Part B at age 65, but during a general enrollment period, your 6 month open enrollment period for Medigap insurance policies begins July 1st of the year you enrolled in Medicare Part B. All Medigap policies are "guaranteed renewable" meaning your policy can't be canceled if you move out of a coverage area, but your premiums may be raised.

Quick Tip: *when researching the many Medigap policy options, be sure to use the "Compare Medigap Policies" section of www.medicare.gov.*

How does Medicare billing work?

Medicare does not handle your day-to-day paperwork and payments. For Medicare Part A, generally you will only receive a bill if (i) there is an unpaid portion of your deductible (ii) any coinsurance payment is due (ex. a hospital inpatient stay of more than 60 days) or (iii) you incur charges not covered at all by Medicare Part A (ex. a private hospital room).

Payment of Medicare Part B expenses are a bit more complex than the payment of Medicare Part A expenses. If assignment is accepted you are responsible for your annual Part B deductible plus the 20% of approved charges Medicare does not pay. By accepting assignment, a doctor agrees not to charge you an amount higher than the amount Medicare approves for your treatment. If a doctor or medical service provider does not accept Medicare assignment then you or any additional medical insurance you own must cover up to an additional 15% of the Medicare approved cost. When you are billed for Medicare Part B expenses, the doctor's office will send all paperwork to Medicare. If you have a Medigap supplemental insurance policy or a Medicare Advantage Plan a bill will be sent to your insurance company as well.

Every three months you will receive a form outlining your Medicare payments called a Medicare Summary Notice. This is not a bill and simply shows how your past claims have been settled. The Medicare Summary Notice will include:

1. Your Medicare intermediary with their contact information. You can contact the intermediary with any questions and appeals you may have after reviewing the Medicare Summary Notice.

2. The type of Medicare claim and the service provided.

3. The division of bills which will include the non-Medicare costs, as well as the Medicare approved cost. The Medicare approved cost is often considerably less than what a non-Medicare patient would have been

charged for the same service. If the doctor or other provider did not accept Medicare part B assignment, the total bill may be higher by as much as 15% of the Medicare approved charges.

Be sure to thoroughly review your Medicare Summary Notice for any issues or mistakes. Contact Medicare, the insurance company that administers your Medicare Plan and your doctor if you have any questions regarding your Medicare Summary Notice.

Quick Tip: you can access sample Medicare Summary Notices at www.medicare.gov.

How do I appeal coverage decisions by my Medicare plan?

Occasionally a Medicare approved hospital or nursing facility review committee will decide your services should not be covered by Medicare Part A (ex. an inpatient hospital stay is too long or not necessary). More commonly, the Medicare carrier will deny Medicare Part B coverage for what you believe is a covered medical service.

Medicare Part A

For Medicare Part A you will receive a notice of non-coverage alerting you of coverage denial. If you disagree, the first thing you should do is contact your doctor and/or hospital. If there is still disagreement over your coverage, your appeal will go to a Peer Review Organization (PRO). It is always wise to verify your appeal actually made it to the PRO. Within three days of your request, the PRO will notify you of their decision in writing. In addition to the PRO, submit your bill to your Medicare intermediary for a review of your appeal. Unfortunately, while your intermediary decides, you may be billed for the services in question. If you win the appeal, Medicare will reimburse you retroactively.

- If your Medicare intermediary denies your appeal, you may request an administrative hearing. A hearing may be requested only if your claim is greater than $100. The form for the administrative hearing request may be accessed on the Social Security website. A letter from your doctor is the most important support you will need for the hearing as well as if you need to move forward further in the appeal process.

- If your appeal is denied by the administrative hearing, the next step is to bring your appeal to the Social Security Appeals Council. If your appeal is again denied, your final step is a challenge in federal court. You can only bring a challenge to federal court if the amount of your claim is more than $1,000.

Medicare Part B The appeal process is quite limited for Medicare Part B as compared to Medicare Part A. Many people have more success informally contacting their Medicare carrier as opposed to undergoing a formal appeals process, particularly for simple mistakes. You can ask your doctor to write a letter of support as to why your treatment was medically necessary and provide this to the carrier as well. If you have not been able to resolve the issue informally, you have 120 days from the date you receive your Medicare Summary Notice to file a written request for redetermination of the carrier's decision. As part of the request, send a marked up copy of your Medical Summary Notice and a signed letter stating your reasons for appeal. In addition, if available, include medical records and a doctor's letter with the request. You will receive a written response from the carrier within 60 days.

- If your request for reconsideration is denied you then have 180 days to contact a Qualified Independent Contractor (QIC) for a decision on your appeal. The contact information for the QIC will be on the written response to your request for redetermination and you will receive a decision notice from the QIC within 60 days.
- If the QIC's decision is negative, and your claim is more than $500, you have 60 days to contact an administrative law judge.
- If your appeal is denied by the administrative law judge the final step you can take is to file a lawsuit in federal court. You are only able to do this if your claim is greater than $1,000.

Medicare Part D The appeals process is extremely important for Medicare Part D because plan medication offerings change so frequently. This means you may begin coverage with a plan that fits your needs only to have the characteristics change. If Medicare Part D changes it can be both financially and physically burdensome for you. If this happens you can request an "exception" from plan rules based on "medical necessity". You make this request to the Medicare Part

D plan itself and not Medicare. You will receive a decision called a "coverage determination" within 72 hours. Your doctor's support is key in this process. If your request for an exception is denied you can file for an appeal. The types of Medicare Part D decisions that can be appealed include:

- Denial of an exception request
- Decision not to cover a drug or only to cover at a higher co-payment
- Decision not to cover a drug because not medically necessary
- Your drug can only be provided by an out-of-network pharmacy

If you receive an unfavorable written coverage determination, you have 60 days to request a "redetermination". Your plan then has 7 days to provide you with a decision. If the redetermination decision is unfavorable you will then contact an Independent Review Entity. If the decision by the Independent Review Entity is unfavorable and your claim is over $100, you have the right to bring your appeal to an administrative law judge. If this too is unfavorable, the next step is to bring your appeal to a Medicare Appeals Council, followed by a federal court appeal. You can only bring your appeal to federal court if it is greater than $1,050.

What happens to my healthcare if I stop working before age 65?

When you stop working before age 65 you may be able to "stretch" your existing health coverage with your employer and avoid medical screening (coverage can be extended for spouse and children as well). The avoidance of medical screening is extremely important if you have an existing illness. Another option is to continue your existing coverage under the Consolidated Omnibus Budget Reconciliation Act (COBRA) which mandates a period of continued health coverage for you if a qualifying event occurs. Qualifying events include (i) death of the covered employee (ii) an employee loses eligibility for coverage due to a reduction in hours (iii) divorce or legal separation that terminates an ex-spouses coverage and (iv) a dependent child reaching the age they are no longer covered. This coverage can be extended to your spouse and children as well. Any termination with regards to COBRA must have been involuntary.

If you qualify, your healthcare can be extended for a few different time periods depending on the qualifying event.
- COBRA allows for 18 months of extended coverage in most cases
- If the Social Security Administration deems you disabled, your coverage may continue for up to 29 months
- If the case is a divorce from a former employee, the spouse's coverage can continue for up to 36 months.
- If the former employee has passed away, the widow/widower may receive coverage for up to 39 months

COBRA does not require the former employer to pay for the cost of continued coverage, instead it allows former employees and their dependents to maintain coverage at the same premium that had previously been paid plus an administrative charge of 2%.

Quick Tip: you can get extensive information on COBRA at
www.healthcare.gov.

What is Medicaid / How do I qualify and apply for Medicaid?

Medicaid is a means-tested program that is jointly funded by both state and federal governments, but managed by the states. States have broad discretion in program implementation as well as in determining Medicaid eligibility. Medicaid is a social health program for families and individuals with low income and limited resources. Those covered may include adults, their children and people with certain disabilities. Poverty alone does not qualify you for Medicaid and you must fall into a certain eligibility category. Medicaid recipients must be U.S. citizens or legal permanent residents. Medicaid eligibility varies from state to state.

Medicaid covers the same types of services as Medicare as well as a number of services Medicare does not. One of the most advantageous features of Medicaid is that it covers most home-based and nursing facility long-term care. This includes not just long-term skilled nursing care, but non-medical personal care such as adult day care and at-home assistance with activities of daily living (ADLs). Medicaid also pays many of the hospital and out-patient bills that Medicare does not such as:

- The inpatient hospital insurance deductible and coinsurance amounts that Medicare does not pay
- The Medicare medical insurance deductible
- The 20% of the Medicare approved doctor's fee that Medicare medical insurance does not pay
- The monthly premium charged for Medicare Part B medical insurance

In every state, Medicaid completely covers certain medical services, paying whatever Medicare does not. These services include:

- Inpatient hospital or skilled nursing facility care

- Nursing home care in approved facilities

- Outpatient hospital or clinic treatment

- Laboratory and X-ray services

- Physicians' services

- Home health care

- Transportation to and from the place you receive medical treatment

State Medicaid programs are not required to cover certain optional medical services. In some cases these services may be covered, but require the Medicaid participant to pay a nominal fee. These optional services include:

- Prescription drugs

- Eye Care

- Dental Care

- Transportation

- Physical therapy

- Prosthetic services

Even if a particular medical service or treatment is covered by Medicaid, you must make sure the care was prescribed by a doctor, administered by a provider that participates in Medicaid and is determined to be medically necessary.

Quick Tip: to see if you qualify for the Medicaid program or to sign up for Medicaid you can go to www.medicaid.gov.

Further Resources

- **www.medicare.gov** – the official website for the U.S. government's Medicare program. This website is a resource that provides official benefit information regarding Medicare including coverage options, costs, preventative services and analysis tools for Medicare benefits.

- **www.shiptacenter.org** – allows state specific access to free one-on-one insurance counseling and assistance for Medicare beneficiaries. Ask any questions or address any concerns you have regarding Medicare.

- **www.ehealthmedicare.com** – note that this is a website run by a private insurer and the information is not verified by Medicare, but the website is an extremely informative resource.

- **www.medicaid.gov** – official Medicaid website run by the U.S. government. This is where you can find out if you qualify for Medicaid, what Medicaid covers and where you can actually sign up for Medicaid.

Books:

- **Medicare & You 2017; Centers for Medicare and Medicaid Services**

  A free publication put out by the government. Great resource that gives a detailed overview of Medicare and Medicaid including benefits, contact information and how to sign up for your benefits.

- **Matthews, Joseph. *Social Security, Medicare & Government Pensions: Get the Most Out of Your Retirement & Medical Benefits.* Nolo. 2017.**

  A reference-style book that helps you figure out your Medicare benefits including how you should apply for and use these benefits. Make sure you have the most recent version of this text.

Chapter 8: Long-term Care Planning

✓ Familiarize yourself with the different types of long-term care facilities and the types of services they provide.

✓ Compare the various financing options you have for long-term care.

✓ Explore the use of long-term care insurance (LTCI), understanding both the benefits and drawbacks of its use.

✓ Execute all other needed "end-of-life" actions.

At some point most of us will find ourselves analyzing the best living situation or a long-term care plan for ourselves or a loved one. This can be a daunting task as numerous programs, places and people are available to help navigate life's later years. These alternatives offer a whole range of care options. Local, state and federal government programs as well as private insurance and finally your own relatives are available to provide care. Before making a decision regarding your options, you will want to understand your financing alternatives, local caregiver resources, and long-term care facilities.

When it comes time to make long-term care arrangements for yourself or someone else, a few basic suggested steps include:

- Locate sources of research and information on alternatives such as home care, independent living, assisted living and nursing homes.

- If needed, find and consult with a geriatric care manager to help you review your long-term care options.

- Decide whether care from a family member or homecare is a possibility.

- Explore residential alternatives to nursing homes, including assisted living and multi-level residential facilities.

- If a nursing home is the appropriate alternative for long-term care, make sure to compare the various services and pricing of each nursing home.

- Periodically asses you or your loved one's particular medical needs. Be sure to look for changes over time as well as for any signs of mental impairment.

How can I research my options for long-term care?

An extremely important aspect of executing a long-term care plan for yourself or a loved one is the initial research you conduct on the numerous options you have available to you. People that can help you as you begin the process of researching long-term care include your personal physician or traditional word-of-mouth suggestions from friends and relatives. As part of your initial research, area aging agencies can provide you with helpful information as can the government's website on aging which can connect you to a counselor or social worker.

Professional geriatric care managers can be used, particularly for at home and supportive services. A geriatric care manager assists in arranging short-term or long-term care. On a one-on-one basis, geriatric care managers can help asses long-term care needs and help you organize services to meet these needs. Geriatric care managers can be invaluable in guiding you through the maze of home healthcare and supporting services. Make sure to check the geriatric care manager's experience and references. Geriatric care managers can charge flat or hourly fees (check the going rate). Be wary of a geriatric care manager that has formal contracts with a long-term care facility.

If you are caring for or aiding loved ones you will want to familiarize yourself with the federal family leave laws, known as the Family Medical Leave Act (FMLA) which must allow 50 days of unpaid time off for a child, spouse or parent. Details are provided by the Department of Labor at 866-487-9243 or www.dol.gov

Quick Tip: you can access the government information on aging and find information on local aging agencies at 1-800-677-1116 or www.eldercare.gov. Use the National Associations of Professional Geriatric care manager's website www.caremanager.org or call 520-881-8008.

What are some of my long-term care alternatives?

Long-term care can consist of a broad array of services that range from permanent care (provides aid with basic activities of daily living) to intensive skilled nursing care during recovery from a serious illness or injury. This care can occur at home or in a nursing facility. There are plenty of long-term care options to help meet the needs of yourself or a loved one. Your needs will be dependent on the state of your health and can change over time. This is why it is good to familiarize yourself with the numerous long-term care facilities and services available to you. Once you've narrowed down your options you should contact or visit the facility or service provider directly.

Home Care

New technologies have made many medical treatments possible at home which can be a less expensive and more comfortable alternative to entering a facility to receive care. Home care can include health care which is provided by a state-licensed health care agency. The homecare agency will typically create a care plan for you that can involve nurses, therapists, social workers and non-professional aides as part of homecare. These care plans should provide detail on all expenses. Home care can often require greater family involvement than other long-term care options, so if you are considering home care, make sure your family has the needed resources. Many people that opt for home care won't need skilled medical care as much as they need assistance with personal tasks because of frailty. If home care will not meet your healthcare needs you will want to explore the care provided at an outside facility. The type of facility will determine the care you receive.

Independent Living Facility

An independent living facility typically has no personal or healthcare services. You rent or purchase an apartment or smaller home in an independent living community. Independent senior living facilities do not provide health care, 24/7 skilled nursing or assistance with activities of daily living (ADLs) such as medication, bathing, eating, dressing, toileting and more. Residents may benefit from convenient services, senior-friendly surroundings, and increased social opportunities that independent senior living communities offer. Independent living facilities are very often used prior to an assisted living facility or a custodial care facility/nursing home and may require a minimum age such as 55. A resident of an independent living facility can often times utilize home healthcare as well.

Assisted Living Facility

The greatest difference between assisted living and independent senior living is the care provided. Residents of assisted living facilities do require assistance with daily activities like medication, eating, bathing, dressing, and toileting. Elderly people who have chosen to live in an assisted retirement complex will often require more care and support to improve their quality of life. Assisted living facilities differ in such details as number of residents, housing style, type of food service, extra amenities, and cost. Licensed facilities provide the basics of all meals, housekeeping, laundry, transportation, recreational activities, and wellness programs. Assisted living offers some health care services, customized to residents' specific needs. Emergency first aid, medication management, pharmacy services, and medical records maintenance services are usually offered to residents. Most facilities also have a staff physician or nurse who visits residents regularly to provide medical checkups.

Nursing Home Facility

A nursing home facility is a residential care facility that provides long-term custodial care. This is different than a skilled nursing facility which provides round-the-clock medical monitoring and daily intensive nursing and therapy. Skilled nursing usually consists of a short-term stay following an injury, illness or surgery. A nursing home facility is a place of residence for people who require continual nursing care and have significant difficulty coping with the required activities of daily living. Nursing aides and skilled nurses are usually available 24 hours a day. Some nursing homes are set up like a hospital. The staff provides medical care, as well as physical, speech and occupational therapy. There might be a nurse's station on each floor. Other nursing homes try to be more like home, with a "neighborhoody" feel. Often, they don't have a fixed day-to-day schedule, and kitchens might be open to residents. Staff members are encouraged to develop relationships with residents. Some nursing homes have special care units for people with serious memory problems such as Alzheimer's disease.

Quick Tips: a **continuing care retirement community** *(sometimes referred to as extended care) is a multilevel facility that allows movement from independent living, assisted living and a nursing facility as needs require. Good general resources on home care and residential care can be found at the Area Total Living Choices website www.tlchoices.com.*

How can I fund long-term care?

A key part of your own or a loved one's long-term care situation is how you finance your long-term care choices. The difficulty many of us face in financing long-term care is that government services and private insurance leave large gaps when it comes to longer-term stays in independent, assisted living or nursing care facilities. It is important to understand the costs you may have to fund yourself because depending on the service, long-term care can be quite expensive.

Adult Day Health Care	
Annual Cost	**Annual Growth**
$18,200	3%

Home Health Care	
Annual Cost	**Annual Growth**
$47,934	3%

Adult Day Health Care	
Annual Cost	**Annual Growth**
$45,000	3%

Nursing Home Care	
Annual Cost	**Annual Growth**
$97,455	4%

Source: Genworth Financial.

Medicare pays only for short-term skilled nursing facility care and does not cover longer-term assisted living, a nursing facility or other residential care. This short-term skilled nursing is usually required during recovery from surgery or a severe injury. In addition, Medicare coverage of short-term skilled nursing is limited.

- Part A of Medicare pays all skilled nursing charges if it is prescribed by a physician and after you pay for your deductible for the first 20 days of care.

- For days 21 through 100 of skilled nursing care, Medicare pays all covered charges except a daily coinsurance amount for which you will be personally responsible.

- After day 100 you are on your own and will be required to fund your skilled nursing care. Unfortunately, Medigap and managed care plans won't provide much more coverage in this area than does Medicare.

Medicaid pays roughly half the country's total nursing facility costs. Once Medicaid kicks in almost all income goes to the long-term care facility and there are federal limits on income and assets you can retain. Unlike Medicare, Medicaid covers the full cost of long-term residence in custodial care nursing homes. In recent years more assisted living facilities have been covered by Medicaid. To qualify for Medicaid, you must file a written application with a local agency, usually the department of social services. Each state has its own standards so check with your county social services agency. You may be able to keep more assets if one spouse stays at home, while the other is in a long-term care facility. When calculating income, you may qualify for Medicaid if your income is initially over the specified income limit, but when medical bills are included you are below the income limit. Exempt assets when you attempt to qualify for Medicaid include a car, furniture, house, a burial plot, wedding and engagement ring. Even if you are able to keep certain assets, Medicaid may be able to seek reimbursement after your death. It is difficult to shift assets to qualify for Medicaid because if there are any large or irregular withdrawals within 60 months prior to your Medicaid application you can be penalized. If applicable, many states have programs in which Medicaid pays a family caregiver.

Long-term care insurance is a potential solution to the care needed later in life, but long-term care insurance is expensive and a bit of a gamble because the odds are you will never need to use it. We review long-term care insurance in detail later in this chapter. If neither government aid or private insurance will cover your long-term care there are some less traditional, alternative methods of raising the needed funds you may want to consider.

- **Reverse mortgage** – a way to convert home equity into cash while remaining in your home. You receive a loan against the value of your home. The loan doesn't have to be repaid until borrower sells or permanently leaves the home. The money is a loan, so it is not taxable as income. You must repay the loan if you sell the home or within 18 months of leaving the property. If your home is sold for more than its cost basis, you can keep the excess, if not, you do not have to cover any shortfall from the sale of your home. Some reverse mortgages are insured by the Federal Housing Administration (FHA). Reverse mortgages are available to homeowner's age 62 or older. Reverse mortgages have serious drawbacks that include high fees, and many restrictions so you should make sure you thoroughly understand the situation prior to entering into any reverse mortgage agreement.

- **Cash in a life insurance policy** – amount you receive will be lower than the face amount of the policy (typically 60% - 80% of the face value). The beneficiary of the life insurance policy will not receive any funds. The process of receiving accelerated life insurance benefits typically requires a treating physician to declare you terminally ill. If you don't qualify for accelerated life insurance benefits, you can explore the sale of your policy to a life settlement company. In a sale to a life settlement company, you will likely receive a lower percentage of the face value and experience a few month delay in the receipt of funds. Be sure to speak with a financial professional prior to entering into such an agreement.

Should I purchase long-term care insurance (LTCI)?

Long-term care insurance (LTCI) is one solution to the rising costs of care needed later in life, but LTCI is expensive and a bit of a gamble because the odds are you will never use it. It is possible you will end up paying LTCI premiums for decades and most policies have extensive restrictions on coverage. In most scenarios, you have to stay multiple years in a facility covered by long-term care for the policy to be worth it. When examining LTCI take into consideration that the likelihood you will need a 2 or 3 year period of care in a long-term residential facility is 30% for men and 15% for women and only 10% to 15% of residents remain in a nursing facility for more than 3 years. A large percentage of policies are not collected until the insured are in their 80s. This can mean decades of premium payments, so be sure any policy has good inflation protection. Most people worry about a long stay in a nursing home, but be aware LTCI can cover home care and assisted living as well.

There really is no simple answer to whether LTCI is a good choice for you. Most consider a LTCI policy as an extra layer of protection for assets if you can afford it. Many experts suggest that LTCI is too risky unless you spend a low level of income (rule of thumb is typically less than 5% of your income should go to LTCI premiums). A certain amount of LTCI premiums can be tax deductible as medical expenses (if your medical expense exceeds 7.5% of AGI). Most policy premiums rise at a certain age. This is why a low level of income is suggested because if premiums become unaffordable, the money you have put towards your LTCI policy will have been wasted. If you do shop for a LTCI policy don't use a single agent or broker, instead seek out as much information from multiple sources as you can. Use your state's department of insurance as a resource. You may be better off with a broker rather than an agent that is limited to selling policies from one company, but get anything a broker says in writing from the insurance company. A LTCI policy will interpret your medical history plus factor in your age.

The older you are, the less likely you will be able to get coverage. Premiums will be higher the older you are. A large concern is if the policy covers a long, expensive stay in a nursing home, so make sure this is broadly defined (no size limitations or Medicare certification needed). Factors taken into consideration when obtaining LTCI include:

- Overall health and health history
- Different types of care covered
- Where you live
- Amount of potential benefits
- Inflation protection
- Marital Status
- Cap on length of premiums

What is Hospice care?

Medical care during the final stages of life can sometimes be invasive and traumatic. Hospice can help with control of patient pain in a comfortable and peaceful setting for the patient and the patient's family. Hospice consists of a coordinated plan with special emphasis put on comfort. Hospice is designed for the last 6 months of a terminal illness and offers physician, nursing, home health care drugs, medical equipment and counseling.

Unlike stays in an independent, assisted living or nursing care facility, Medicare Part A, Medicaid and private health insurance all offer hospice coverage. Although the majority of Hospice care is covered, you will still have to pay:

- a small amount of drug prescriptions
- respite care while inpatient care is used

Due to the extensive low-cost coverage offered, you should consider Hospice at the appropriate time. To receive Hospice care, a physician must certify you have a life expectancy of 6 months. This part of the process can be difficult for all parties involved because to receive Hospice care you must give up the option to receive life prolonging treatment. You can always switch back to your previous Medicare treatment from Hospice care though. You can only receive Hospice care from a Medicare approved program. Much of Hospice care is performed by specially trained nurses, but a Hospice physician will oversee your care plan. Therapists and dieticians can be involved in your Hospice care as well. Hospice directly provides you with all medical supplies without the need for a doctor's prescription. A Hospice care plan will usually include respite care provided for up to a few days at a time to give the patient's family a break. You will work with a specific Hospice care agency that coordinates with treating physicians, family and other caregivers. To formally enroll, your treating physician will fill out a Medicare document on your prognosis and you will sign a document confirming that you will give up Medicare coverage. Hospice care is analyzed after 90 days and then every 60 days thereafter.

What other "end-of-life" legal actions should I execute?

When considering your long-term care needs, it is an ideal time to review other legal and financial matters that will become important towards the end of your life. These matters include executing a living will and durable powers of attorney.

Your living will is a health care declaration that states your wishes about life support and other kinds of medical treatment. The document takes effect if you can't communicate these wishes yourself. A durable power of attorney appoints an "attorney-in-fact" or "health-care proxy" to ensure you get the medical care you wish to receive. You don't necessarily need a lawyer to execute these documents and it's a good idea to use your state's specific forms. You can access these documents by contacting a local senior center, doctor or hospital or you can go to the "End of Life" section of the AARP website at www.aarp.org. Some states have you fill out an Advanced Health Care Directive which incorporates both a living will and a durable power of attorney. The person you appoint can make decisions on your behalf including:

- Withholding and withdrawing consent to medical or surgical procedures
- Consent to appropriate care for end of life including pain relief
- Hiring and firing medical personnel
- Obtaining access to medical records
- Taking any legal action necessary

A durable power of attorney for finances allows you to name an "attorney-in-fact" to handle financial affairs for you if you are unable to. This attorney-in-fact can do such things as use assets to pay everyday expenses, collect benefits from Social Security and Medicare, invest funds in various securities on your behalf, represent you in court and manage your retirement accounts.

Further Resources

- **www.longtermcare.gov** – government website that provides a very good overview of long-term care insurance including care options and how to best fund this care.

- **www.longtermcareinsurance.org** – helps you to compare costs based on the region you live in and the type of care you require. Allows you to download a Care Planning Guide and a Care Planning Checklist to help organize your research and decision-making process.

- **www.aarp.org** – website that caters to retirees. Keyword search "long-term care" to get useful information and current articles on long-term care.

- **www.nahc.org** – National Association for Home Care & Hospice website that maintains a list of home care agencies and offers a guide to making a home care and/or hospice choice.

Books:

- **Genworth: Cost of Care Survey 2017**

  Genworth is a large provider of long-term care insurance that produces an unbiased annual survey on long-term care. The survey is a good starting point to get an overview of long-term care services and the cost of these services. You can download the survey at www.genworth.com.

- **Matthews, Joseph L.** *Long-term care: How to Plan & Pay for It.* **Nolo. 2016.**

  Helps you to understand the range of possible long-term care choices as well as how to get the most out of the various funding alternatives. Make sure you have the most up to date version of this text.

Chapter 9: My Estate Plan

✓ Regardless of the size of your estate, put together a will to specify who gets your property when you die and appoints a personal guardian to raise your children.

✓ Seek ways to avoid probate, the often time-consuming and expensive court-run process for wrapping up your estate.

✓ Plan for a time you are unable to make medical or financial decisions for yourself by setting up a health care directive and durable power of attorney.

✓ If you will be subject to estate taxes explore the various avenues available to reduce the value of your estate.

Estate planning is for everyone, regardless of your net worth or financial situation. The idea of estate planning can be intimidating and yes, certain parts of estate planning can be complex, but other elements of estate planning are quite simple and will be essential to your financial planning process.

The tools of estate planning make sure that your property will efficiently pass to the people you wish. If you have young children, an estate plan ensures that your children are cared for if you are not around. You can use estate planning to leave specific instructions for others about your finances and medical care if you are ever in a position where you are unable to make these types of decisions yourself.

Estate planning can't be reduced to one universal formula. There are numerous variables including the size of your estate, the type of assets in your estate, where you live, as well as the number and age of any dependents you have. Estate planning choices are not always clear cut because emotional issues involving family and close acquaintances can come into play.

When it comes to estate planning, a trusted lawyer, accountant or financial advisor can all be a great resource for your questions regarding more complex issues. Although you may employ professionals specializing in estate planning it is a good idea to gain a working knowledge of the topic yourself. This will help you limit any fees you pay and maintain better control of your own estate planning situation.

Quick Tip: There is much greater detail on estate planning including estate and gift taxes on the IRS website. This publication designed for executors is particularly helpful https://www.irs.gov/pub/irs-pdf/p559.pdf.

What can I accomplish through the estate planning process?

Estate planning is the process of accumulation, management, conservation, and transfer of wealth, while considering legal, tax and personal objectives. It is essential that as part of the estate planning process you set your own goals, perform diligence on your estate planning options and work with trusted professionals if need be. Successful estate planning can help you accomplish the following.

- **Leaving property**

  There are numerous ways to leave property to those you wish to have it. If you are leaving property to a spouse, take advantage of the unlimited marital deduction and portability of the federal tax exemption. If you have a more modest estate, you can use a simple will and/or a living trust. In addition, you should be sure that your assets are in appropriate co-ownership account types. If your estate is larger, you may want to explore the use of more complex ongoing trusts.

- **Avoiding probate**

  Probate is the often time-consuming and expensive court-run process for wrapping up your estate (a good estimate is 5% of estate value and 6 months). Bypassing probate can be fairly easy through the use of pay-on-death accounts, joint tenancy, and other probate avoidance methods though.

- **Providing for children**

  In a will, you name guardians to raise your children in the event that you aren't around. You can name managers to watch over any wealth your children may inherit. This is important as minors are only allowed to own a minimal level of assets. In addition, you may want to have sufficient life insurance to cover the future needs of your children.

- **Planning for incapacity**

Estate planning provides tools to prepare for a time you are unable to make medical or financial decisions for yourself. You can use a health care directive to name someone to make medical decisions on your behalf and express your wishes regarding end-of-life care. For your finances, you can prepare a durable power of attorney to give a trusted person control of your finances.

- **Reducing estate tax**

Due to the changes enacted as part of the Tax Relief, Unemployment Insurance Reauthorization and Job Creation Act of 2010, most people won't owe estate tax until the value of your estate reaches at least a few million dollars based on current estate tax thresholds. If your estate is large enough, you may be subject to estate taxes at a 40% tax rate. Your estate plan might incorporate such tools as marital trusts, charitable trusts or life insurance trusts. If this is the case, you should definitely look into working with an estate planning professional.

Why should I create a will and how do I do so?

You should have a will, no matter how basic or extensive your estate planning may be. A will is a legal document that specifies who gets your property when you die and can be used to appoint a personal guardian to raise your children. Property left by will normally goes through probate. Probate is the court process by which a will is proved valid or invalid and probate procedures are dictated by state law. Probate can be costly and burdensome. In addition, the process makes the contents of your will public which may be uncomfortable for you and your family. Luckily there are a number of ways to avoid probate. We provide further detail on the probate process and ways to avoid probate later in this chapter. Probate avoidance devices can't take care of all asset distribution for you though, which is just one of the reasons it's still important to have a will. Other reasons to create a will include:

- A will can cover your basic estate planning needs and allow you to postpone more complicated and costly estate planning measures, especially if you don't have an extensive asset base.

- In many states naming a personal or property guardian for your children if you die can only be done through a will.

- A will can help you to efficiently pass along property you don't currently own, but expect to receive in the future.

- If you wish to, a will is the only way to expressly disinherit a child.

- A will and the probate process will provide an organized forum in which to deal with any creditors you have and limit the timeframe in which your creditors can bring claims against you.

- A will allows you to name an executor, who will be responsible for seeing your will through the probate process as well as take on other responsibilities such as filing a federal estate tax return if needed.

To legally create a will you must be at least 18 years old and of sound mind. You must appoint an executor in your will and sign your will in front of two witnesses that are also over 18 and of sound mind. Note that your witnesses can't be beneficiaries of the will. It is recommended that you type your will and keep the original copy in a safe place.

What is probate and how can I avoid it?

When you die, your estate must go through probate. Probate proceedings will usually be held in a local court (surrogate court) in the state in which you lived. If you have a will directing how your property should be distributed at death, the probate court must determine if it should be admitted to probate and given legal effect (basically, approved). As the creator of the will, you are known as the "testator". If you die without creating a will, it is known as "intestate" and the court will appoint its own representative to distribute your property according to state laws which may or may not have been how you wished to allocate your property.

The probate process begins when your personal representative, likely the executor you name in your will, files with the clerk of the probate court a copy of your death certificate, along with the will (should be the original copy), a petition to admit the will and a petition to grant letters of testamentary which will ultimately allow the representative to distribute the estate. Unless an informal probate proceeding is used (which can benefit smaller estates), a hearing will be held to establish your death, residency, genuineness of the will and conformance with statutory requirements. This is usually fulfilled by the witnesses at the time your will was created (if a witness is deceased your representative should provide the death certificate). If no one objects to your will at the hearing, it will be admitted to probate and the distribution of your assets can begin.

When the process is summed up in a few paragraphs, probate doesn't seem so bad, but probate can truly be a pain for those you leave behind and can put a sizable dent in the value of your assets through administrative and professional fees. This is why although you should still have a will for the reasons we've discussed, you should attempt to limit your assets that are eventually subject to probate. To avoid probate, you should maximize the use of assets subject to contract or assets that you pass on through operation of law.

(i) Assets passing by contract

• Life insurance proceeds with a valid named beneficiary

• Retirement plans with valid named beneficiaries

• Annuities with named joint annuitants

• Pay-on-death and transfer-on-death accounts

(ii) Assets passing by operation of law

• Assets titled Joint Tenancy with Rights of Survivorship

• Property titled as tenants by entirety

• Trust property – both revocable and irrevocable trusts created inter vivos (during life)

What is the estate tax and what is the gift tax?

Estate tax is based on the value of your gross estate when you die. Your gross estate consists of the assets in which you have an interest at the time of your death. Certain property you don't "own" can increase the value of your gross estate. For instance, property transferred within three years of your death or in which you retained a reversionary interest. The IRS website provides a comprehensive list of these gross estate additions.

Gifting: understanding the "gifting" concept is extremely important, especially if you have an estate large enough to be subject to estate taxes. Each year you can gift a certain amount (in 2018 this amount is $15,000) to another individual without incurring any tax. This gift permanently reduces the value of your estate that will be subject to estate tax. If you "split" the gift with your spouse, the amount you can provide to the same individual tax-free doubles to $30,000. If gift-splitting is used your spouse will need to provide consent via IRS form 709. Although your gift to one individual can't exceed the thresholds previously outlined, you can provide gifts to more than one individual (ex. if gift-splitting is used, you can provide a husband and wife $30,000 each in any one year). Any amount above this annual gift exemption is classified as an "adjusted taxable gift" and will be added to the value of your estate when you die.

Once you have an idea of what the value of your gross estate is, you deduct from this any outstanding debts and expenses such as mortgages and lines of credit. In addition, prior to any application of estate tax, you can make other selected deductions including funeral expenses, the administrative costs of winding up your estate and certain charitable contributions you make.

Now is the part where the majority of us will avoid paying any sort of estate tax. The reasons for this avoidance are (i) the unlimited marital deduction (ii) a hefty federal estate tax exemption and (iii) the portability of this estate tax exemption as explained below.

- **Federal Estate Tax Exclusion and Portability** – in 2017, the estate and gift tax exclusion is $5,490,000 and only amounts above this will be taxed. In addition, if you are married, each spouse has a $5,490,000 exclusion which the "portability" concept allows to be passed to a surviving spouse if unused. This means the estate of a surviving spouse must exceed $10,980,000 before they experience any estate taxes. In 2018, due to the terms of the Tax Cuts and Jobs Act of 2017 the terms of the Federal Estate Tax Exclusion and Portability is even more advantageous with limits increasing to $11.2 million for each individual and $24.4 million for a couple.

- **Unlimited Marital Deduction** – no taxes are paid on assets transferred to your surviving spouse. This means that any assets you transfer to your spouse, no matter the value will avoid estate tax and continue to accrue value.

Estate tax rates are high with a rate of 40% applied to amounts in excess of the Federal Estate Tax Exclusion. Many states, including New York apply more modest taxes to sizable estates, so be sure to inquire about your state's estate taxes. We have provided a summary of estate and gift taxes, but in the event these taxes may apply to your estate, definitely consult an estate planning or tax expert.

Quick Tips: to define "permanently reduces value of the estate" lets use an oversimplified example. If your estate is $30,000 above the threshold for estate taxation and you make a $30,000 gift, you will reduce the value of your estate and pay no estate taxes. The New York State estate tax exemption can be found here https://tax.ny.gov/pit/estate/etidx.htm and every state will have their own estate tax rules.

What are the best ways to leave property to a minor?

Leaving property to your minor children can be tricky. Most states only allow a minor to own minimal amounts of property, usually between $2,500 and $5,000 depending on the state. In addition, the "kiddie tax" eliminates the incentive for parents to transfer assets to their lower-taxed children. The kiddie tax kicks in only when your child's investment income exceeds $2,100. The first $1,050 reported on your return is tax free, the second $1,050 is taxed at the child's lower tax rate. Unearned income above that amount is subject to your marginal tax rate.

When you pass along assets to a child, you will have to appoint an adult to control property on behalf of the child. The terms most commonly applied to the adult legally responsible for the assets are "custodian", "trustee" or "property guardian" depending on the type of account you use. Despite these restrictions, there are still a number of ways to provide assets to your children, two of the most common and popular ways of doing this are either a Uniform Transfers to Minors Account (UTMA) or a child's trust.

- **Uniform Transfers to Minors Account (UTMA)**
  Custodial accounts that are set up by an adult on behalf of a minor. You can set up a UTMA yourself through any number of the popular financial services companies (Fidelity, TD Ameritrade etc.). When setting up this type of account, you choose a minor as the beneficiary of the assets and an adult as the custodian. The custodian's management responsibilities end and the minor has full access to the assets between the ages of 18 and 25 depending on the state law that applies (check for your states age). A UTMA is taxed at the child's rate, but is subject to the Kiddie Tax. A UTMA can reduce your child's eligibility for college financial aid, but unlike other ways of saving for college offers investment freedom (529 Investment Plans generally limit your investment choices).

- **Child's Trust**

   When you create a child's trust, the property manager is known as the "trustee". A child's trust can be a living trust (not subject to probate) or established in a will (subject to probate). The assets in the trust are subject to less advantageous trust tax rates. The key advantage of a child's trust is that there is no age limitation that requires the minor be given access to the assets. If you want to set up a child's trust you should consult an estate planning professional.

Quick Tip: your marginal tax rate is essentially the tax rate you will pay on one additional dollar of income. In many cases, you can report your child's investment income on your tax return (using IRS Form 8814).

How can I pass someone else control of my medical and financial affairs if I'm incapacitated?

Defining estate planning as the arrangement of important matters when you die is a bit too narrow. You must consider the fact you may be physically and/or mentally incompetent during life. If this were ever to be the case, you need to be able to protect your rights and control your property. If you do nothing to prevent such a situation, court proceedings will be required to handle your medical and financial issues. With no documents in place, your descendants or someone else on your behalf will have to apply for guardianship or financial conservatorship through the court. These court proceedings will be less than desirable and potentially very costly.

The U.S. Supreme Court has held that every individual has the right to control their own medical care and every state authorizes individuals to create simple documents stating their medical wishes. Your living will is a health care declaration that states your wishes about life support and other kinds of medical treatment. The document takes effect if you can't communicate these wishes yourself. A durable power of attorney appoints an "attorney-in-fact" or "health-care proxy" to ensure you get the medical care you wish to receive. When it comes to a durable power of attorney or advanced medical directives, it's a good idea to use your states specific forms. Some states have you fill out an Advanced Health Care Directive which incorporates both a living will and a durable power of attorney. The person you appoint can make decisions on your behalf including:

- Withholding and withdrawing consent to medical or surgical procedures
- Consenting to appropriate care for end of life actions including pain relief
- Hiring and firing medical personnel
- Obtaining access to medical records

• Taking any legal action necessary

A durable power of attorney for finances allows you to name an "attorney-in-fact" to handle financial affairs for you if you are unable to. This attorney-in-fact can do such things as use assets to pay everyday expenses, collect benefits from Social Security and Medicare, invest funds in various securities on your behalf, represent you in court and manage your retirement accounts.

You should discuss the above documents with your doctor and make sure that they have a copy of these documents on hand. Your living will and durable power of attorney can take effect immediately or you can have them be "springing". Springing means that a doctor must certify you are incapacitated. Verify the process with your state, but many states require that you sign the documents in the presence of a notary and may require witnesses. You can change your living will, durable power of attorney or attorney-in-fact at any time, but you must do this formally and destroy your old documents.

Quick Tip: *you can access living will and durable power of attorney forms by contacting a local senior center, doctor or hospital or you can go to the "End of Life" section of the AARP website at www.aarp.org.*

What are some types of trusts I might be able to use?

Trusts and their use are one of the most, if not the most complex concepts in estate planning. Here we provide only a brief summary of the concept of a trust as well as a few of the trusts available for your use. Definitely contact a professional prior to implementing a trust.

A trust is a legal arrangement that involves three parties (i) The grantor (settlor) transfers the property, called principal or corpus, into the trust. (ii) The trustee holds legal title to the assets and has a fiduciary responsibility to safeguard and distribute the assets. (iii) The beneficiary is the person that receives the benefit of the trust. It is not always necessary for three different individuals to be involved as one individual can serve two or more of these functions. A beneficiary can receive an interest in either the ongoing income or remaining assets of the trust. The duration of a trust can vary, but there is a rule that prevents trusts from having an infinite life (note this rule does not apply to charitable trusts). There are a number of reasons you may want to create a trust including:

- The avoidance of probate
- To avoid/reduce estate taxes
- Maintenance of asset management in the case you are incapacitated
- To make a charitable contribution while retaining some interest in trust assets

A trust can either be revocable or irrevocable. A revocable trust is able to be rescinded or amended by the grantor. An irrevocable trust is one in which the grantor has given up all control of the property and can make no additional changes. A funded trust has property placed in it, while an unfunded trust is legally ready to receive property but has not yet done so. The distribution of trust property allows grantors to elect one of a few options. A special or limited power of appointment allows the trustee to invade trust principal only for health, education, maintenance or support purposes. General powers of appointment allow the trustee the power to appoint trust income or principal to satisfy beneficiary or estate creditors for any reason. If a trust is treated as a separate taxable entity, the trustee will file IRS Form 1041 on or before April 15th following the applicable tax year.

There are numerous trusts you can utilize in your estate planning process. We have categorized and summarized a few of them here. If you think that one of these trusts may be useful to you, you should consult a professional before taking action yourself.

Marital Trusts:

Qualified Terminal Interest Property (QTIP) Trust – Allows interest to be passed to a surviving spouse and the property to still qualify for the marital deduction. Power is provided to the grantor to name who ultimately receives the assets. Creation of the QTIP is accomplished through an election made by the executor on IRS Form 706. All income must be payable to a surviving spouse at least annually for life. Assets will be placed in a QTIP so that income supports your spouse throughout their life with remaining assets typically going to your children (as opposed to a new spouse, step-children etc.). This type of trust is popular in second marriages. The value of the assets are included in the surviving spouses gross estate for estate tax purposes.

Power of Appointment Trust – Often times known as "Trust A". Very similar to the QTIP trust with the key difference being the rights given to your spouse. In a Power of Appointment Trust, the spouse is given power (as opposed to the grantor) to name who receives the trust's assets. The spouse can choose a new spouse, step-children or whomever to receive trust assets. All income must be payable to a surviving spouse at least annually for life. Assets are included in the surviving spouse's estate, but your spouse is able to give away assets during their lifetime as a gift.

Bypass Trust – Often times known as "Trust B". Purpose is to take advantage of the applicable credit amount when the first spouse dies. The appeal of this type of trust has been greatly diminished due to the portability of the estate tax exemption. Not a great deal of difference from an outright transfer of assets aside from the extra control provided to the grantor. The assets are included in the first decedent spouse's estate, freezing the value and bypassing the surviving spouse's gross estate.

Qualified Domestic Trust (QDOT) – the unlimited marital deduction is disallowed if your surviving spouse is not a U.S. citizen. You can give your non-U.S. citizen spouse gifts at an elevated level of $152,000 per year (as opposed to the $15,000 annual gifting limit) during the course of your lifetime. If you are married to a non-citizen, a QDOT is the only way in which you can qualify for the unlimited marital tax deduction and defer estate tax until the death of the spouse.

Qualified Interest Trusts:

Grantor Retained Trust (GRAT or GRUT) – grantor transfers property to the trust and retains qualified income interest for the term of the trust (many times a shorter-term of 2 to 5 years). Remaining assets pass to family members at end of trust term. A GRAT or GRUT allows you the opportunity to transfer assets while retaining an interest in them. Income is taxed to grantor during trust term. The value of the gift at trust creation is the Fair Market Value of property minus the value of your retained interest. The GRAT provides you with a fixed annual payment while the GRUT provides you with a set percentage payment each year. If you die during the trust term the assets will be included in your estate, while if you outlive the trust the assets will not be included in your estate.

Qualified Personal Residence Trust (QPRT) – Grantor transfers personal residence to a trust and retains the right to live in the residence during the trust term. The residence passes to family members at the end of the trust term thus avoiding probate. The grantor may repurchase or rent the residence if the grantor outlives the trust term. The income is taxed to the grantor during the trust term. The value of the gift at trust creation is the Fair Market Value of the residence for the number of years of the trust term at the applicable IRS Section 7520 rate. The gift is of future interest and does not qualify for the annual exclusion.

Charitable Trusts:

Charitable Remainder Annuity Trust (CRAT) – a split interest gift that is usually created during your life where the donor receives a fixed annuity and the remainder goes to charity. The contributions to the trust are made at set up only. The grantor receives an annuity interest of at least 5% of the original value of the trust's assets. Term can be for life or a term of up to 20 years. The present value of the remainder interest must be at least 10% of the initial Fair Market Value of initial assets. A donor is eligible for an immediate charitable contribution for income tax purposes subject to limitations on the type of charity and donor's Adjusted Gross Income (AGI).

Charitable Remainder Uniform Trust (CRUT) – a split interest gift where part of the interest is given to charity. The donor receives a variable annuity with the remainder going to charity. Contributions after the initial setup are permitted. The grantor must receive payment of at least 5% of the current fair market value of the assets. This type of trust appeals to those wishing to hedge against inflation (due to the variable payment). The donor is eligible immediately for a charitable contribution deduction for income tax purposes. If the trust is created during your lifetime, the trust is subject to Adjusted Gross Income (AGI).

Pooled Income Fund (PIF) – an investment fund created and maintained by the target charity. Pools property from all contributors and pays a return based on the fund's earnings. Sometimes limitations are placed on investments and the fund may limit donations to cash. PIFs are frequently maintained by colleges and universities and preferred by those who may not want to establish a trust. The donor is eligible for an immediate charitable contribution deduction for income tax purposes. If the trust is created during your lifetime, the deduction is subject to Adjusted Gross Income (AGI) limitations.

Charitable Lead Trust (CLAT or CLUT) – property is transferred to a trust that distributes income to a charitable beneficiary for a specific term with the remaining assets reverting to a non-charitable beneficiary. This beneficiary can be the grantor, spouse, child or someone else. May be good if you have a large amount of appreciated assets and all other needs are taken care of. If it is a grantor trust, the grantor is taxed on the income and is eligible for a charitable deduction equal to the amount the trust pays to the charity subject to limitations on the type of charity and your AGI. If the trust is a non-grantor trust you can't receive an income tax deduction.

How can a living trust help to accomplish my estate planning goals?

We previously reviewed numerous types of trusts that you can use as part of your estate planning, but we chose to examine living trusts in a bit more detail due to their popularity and usefulness in avoiding probate. Probate is the court supervised process of paying your debts and distributing your property to those who are going to inherit it. Probate can eat up the value of this property through legal and administrative fees. In addition, the probate process can take an extensive amount of time.

This is where a living trust comes in, through the avoidance of probate and probate fees. The property you transfer into a living trust before your death doesn't go through probate. The successor trustee you appoint to handle the trust after your death can simply transfer ownership to the beneficiaries you name in your living trust without the hassles and expense of probate.

To construct a basic living trust, you create a document called a declaration of trust which is similar to a will. You name yourself as the trustee, the person in charge of trust property. You can name a co-trustee as well (such as a spouse). You then transfer ownership of the property you want to include in your living trust to yourself as trustee. For example, to transfer your home you might sign a deed transferring the house to yourself as "trustee of the John Smith Revocable Trust dated October 27, 2018". You have now given up control over the property that you put in the trust. In the trust document you will name the people or organizations you want to inherit the trust property after your death. When you die, the person you named successor trustee will transfer the ownership of the trust property to the appropriate parties.

Along with the avoidance of probate, one of the appeals of a living trust is the ease with which a living trust can be created. Although making a living trust takes about the same amount of time and effort as a will, it can be a quite a bit more complicated. So, despite the ease of creating a living trust, it is a good idea to contact an estate planning professional with questions.

What role can life insurance play in estate planning?

Life insurance has long been part of estate planning and can be used to solve a number of common estate planning problems including:

- Providing immediate cash at death to pay debts, funeral expenses and estate tax. Note that any estate tax will not be payable until nine months after your death.

- The avoidance of probate. Life insurance passes straight to your named beneficiary.

- If you do not legally own your policy, the proceeds of your life insurance policy will not be part of your estate and not subject to estate tax.

When deciding how much life insurance you may need, you should analyze how much liquidity is required both shorter and longer-term. The number of dependents you have and their ongoing cash needs will determine your longer-term insurance requirements. In the shorter-term, the immediate liquidity required to pay off any debts, administrative costs from settling your probate or cash needed to sustain a business will determine your insurance requirements.

In general, you can break insurance into term insurance and permanent insurance. Term insurance is coverage for a certain period that provides you with a pre-set amount of cash if you die while your policy is in force. If you live beyond the term of the policy, you will receive nothing. The premiums you pay for a term policy do not build up, so there are no reserves to invest. For this reason term policies are cheaper than permanent life insurance policies and are generally more suitable for younger consumers. Permanent insurance lasts for the course of your entire life and is renewable without a physical exam. A portion of your premium goes into a reserve account that is then invested on your behalf.

Remember if you are going to name a minor as the beneficiary of your life insurance they will be unable to receive and manage the proceeds themselves. You will have to either have the court appoint a property guardian or form a trust which will receive the insurance proceeds and name the minor as the beneficiary of the trust.

There are a couple types of life insurance policies you may find particularly useful in estate planning. Survivorship life insurance also known as a "second-to-die" or a "joint" life insurance policy allows the policy holder to collect proceeds only on the death of the second holder. This means that the proceeds will be received at the time when estate taxes may be due. A first-to-die life insurance policy is most often used by those that own businesses. The proceeds of the policy will be used by the remaining business owners to purchase the ownership stake of the owner that passed away. If you want to use these policies, be sure to consult not only a life insurance professional, but an estate planning professional to make sure you will have the coverage that you intend.

As part of an estate plan, you can transfer your life insurance policy to another party so that they are able to receive the proceeds. There are two ways you can do this. The first is just to simply transfer it to the other party. You can do this by working with your insurance company which will provide you with the proper paperwork. When you transfer the policy you lose all power over it forever. If however, you maintain the ability to borrow, surrender, cancel or select payment options on your policy it will remain as part of your estate when you die. If the transfer is made within three years of your death your policy will be included in your estate as well. When you are transferring your policy, if it has a present value above the gift tax limit you may owe gift tax.

The other way you may transfer your insurance policy is by creating an irrevocable life insurance trust. Such a trust is a legal entity you create while you are alive for purposes of owning life insurance that you previously owned personally. The trust must be irrevocable, and you can't serve as the trustee. The trust must be established within three years of your death or your insurance policy will still be included in your estate.

When contemplating whether to include insurance as part of your estate plan, make sure you actually need insurance (you may have sufficient liquidity without the use of insurance) and if you do use insurance in your estate plan, be sure you know what you are purchasing. Insurance policies can have high premiums so educate yourself and consult with knowledgeable financial professionals you trust. In addition, you can consult with your state department of insurance with any questions and obtain sample premiums from a reputable online service.

Quick Tip: *a good resource when you are looking into life insurance options is the National Association of Insurance Commissioners website http://naic.org/.*

What post-death actions will be important for me to take care of?

Post-death decisions can be unpleasant to think about and to discuss, but the more you communicate about this with those you trust, the better off both you and those you leave behind will be. Funerals can be expensive and one of the first funeral-related decisions you will have to make is what to do with your body. Traditional funeral services by a commercial funeral home allow you the option of either a cremation or burial. If you have any preference at all, you may want to make arrangements yourself. If you leave no instruction, your next of kin will be responsible to make decisions regarding your body. In addition to commercial funeral providers, you can look in to non-profit funerals or funeral memorial societies as an alternative.

Commercial funerals remain extremely popular and generally as part of their services offer:

- Taking care of paperwork associated with death
- Obtaining the body for you and embalming the body
- Showing the body

If you want to be buried, you will want to contact the cemetery you desire. Most cemeteries are private and will charge you for the plot, coffin, opening/closing of your grave and upkeep. In addition, prior to your death you may want to speak to whomever you deem responsible for your obituary on what you would like written about you (some people choose to write a few things themselves prior to death) and where you would like these words to appear.

You should organize all records your descendants will need to access and keep a number of copies with your doctor. You should provide another few copies with other people you trust. Your descendants will need to access to your death certificate and can obtain this from your physician who is required to file it.

Descendants should contact the insurance company or companies where you have any outstanding policies. They can submit a claim and obtain proceeds from any policies you have. If there is a delay in obtaining these proceeds for any reason your descendants can contact their state insurance commissioner. Finally, it is a good idea to leave the contact information for any lawyer, accountant or other financial professional you use with the person that will be responsible for your post-death matters.

Further Resources

- **www.kiplinger.com** – Kiplinger has an extensive estate planning section on its website. There are a number of useful articles and white papers available for you to download as well.
- **www.irs.gov** – the official Internal Revenue Service website can be a little dry, but has great information on estate and gift taxes, including Publication 559 which is useful for anyone that has to wind up an estate (an executor).
- **www.aarp.org** – the aarp website has a very informative "End of Life" section that provides a useful estate planning checklist and multiple forms.

Books:

Donaldson, Samuel A. and Price, John R. *Price on Contemporary Estate Planning*. CCH, a Wolters Kluwer business. 2016.
Extremely comprehensive estate planning resource. Covers all relevant topics and has highly useful ready-to-adapt forms and checklists.

Clifford, Denis. *Plan Your Estate*. Nolo. 2017.
A reference-style book that helps you understand your estate planning options and execute the proper estate plan. Focuses more on the legal aspects of estate planning.

Peragine, John N. Jr. *Organizing Your Records for Estate Planning*. Atlantic Publishing Group, Inc. 2009.
Designed to help simplify the process of organizing your records for estate planning purposes. Doing this will help you to limit the time and money you spend with estate planning professionals.

Soled, Jay A. *The ABA (American Bar Association) Practical Guide to Estate Planning.* **American Bar Association, Senior Lawyers Division.**

Will help to guide you to the most effective estate plan to fit your needs. Interesting feature of the book is the first-hand accounts and examples provided by professional estate planners. Be sure to find the most updated addition of this text.

APPENDIX A: TAX DETAIL

The General Tax Equation is below along with detail on each part of the equation. We only list a portion of the exclusions and deductions used in calculating your Taxable Income, so be sure to check the IRS website (https://www.irs.gov/) if you want all available information. This is especially important given the changes brought about by the Tax Cuts and Jobs Act of 2017.

General Income Tax Equation
Income (broadly conceived)
Less: Exclusions from Gross Income
Gross Income
Less: Deductions for Adjusted Gross Income (AGI)
Adjusted Gross Income
Less: Greater of (i) Itemized Deductions or (ii) Standard Deduction
Less: Personal and dependency exemptions
Taxable Income

Source: *Internal Revenue Service (IRS)*

I. Income (broadly conceived)

The calculation of Gross Income is not limited simply to the wages you receive from an employer as reported on your W2 Form. Gross Income can include a number of other inflows including:

- Gains from investments sold prior to a 1 year holding period
- Non-qualified interest and dividends on your investments
- If you are part of a partnership, your pass-through income
- Unemployment proceeds
- Up to 85% of your Social Security receipts

II. Exclusions from Gross Income

Only items that are specifically laid out in the tax code are excludable from gross income. Generally, the items excluded from gross income are either donative in nature, a return of capital, or socially desirable. Once these items are taken away from your income the result is your Gross Income. These exclusions can include among other items:

- Gifts, bequests and inheritances you receive
- Scholarships for tuition and books
- Life insurance proceeds paid to you
- Certain employer-provided benefits
- Accelerated death benefits including the gain on the sale of a life insurance policy
- Interest on state and local government obligations
- Certain gains from the ownership of small business stock
- Income from discharge of indebtedness
- Certain gains resulting from the sale of a personal residence

III. Deductions for Adjusted Gross Income (AGI)

These are often referred to as "above-the-line" deductions which are subtracted from your Gross Income to arrive at Adjusted Gross Income (AGI). The importance of Adjusted Gross Income is explained below.

- If you are self-employed, you can deduct a portion of self-employment tax.
- Alimony paid to an ex-spouse (this deduction is eliminated starting in 2018 as part of the Tax Cuts and Jobs Act of 2017).
- Traditional IRA contributions (deductibility based on AGI level).
- Certain moving expenses (this deduction is eliminated starting in 2018 as part of the Tax Cuts and Jobs Act of 2017).
- Any interest penalty for the premature withdrawal of a Certificate of Deposit.

- Excess capital losses (can be used to offset up to $3,000 of ordinary income).
- Contributions to Health Savings Accounts (HSAs).
- Student loan interest (deductibility based on Modified AGI levels).

IV. Adjusted Gross Income (AGI)

Adjusted Gross Income (AGI) is not the value your tax rate will be applied to, but it is an important subtotal because it serves as the amount for calculating percentage limitations for various taxable deductions, credits, phase outs and penalties. For further detail on AGI and how its calculated, check the IRS website.

- Itemized charitable deductions can't be greater than 50% of AGI.
- Itemized medical expenses must exceed 10% of your AGI before deductions can be taken. The Tax Cuts and Jobs Act of 2017 changed this percentage from 10% to 7.5% for two years starting in 2018.
- Miscellaneous itemized deductions must exceed 2% of your AGI before deductions can be taken.
- The ability to exclude income from educational savings bonds is limited by AGI levels.
- The ability to contribute to a Coverdell Education Savings account, take the American Opportunity Tax Credit or take the Lifetime Learning Credit is phased out based on your AGI.
- The ability to deduct contributions to a Traditional IRA account is phased out based on your AGI.
- Your ability to make contributions to a Roth IRA is phased out based on your AGI.
- The deductibility of your student loan interest is based on Modified AGI levels.
- There is a limitation on Itemized Deductions if your AGI exceeds certain limits. Allowable itemized deductions are reduced by 3% of the amount

your AGI exceeds a specific threshold, but the total reduction can't exceed 80% of your itemized deductions.

– There is an overall limitation on your ability to claim personal and dependency exemptions if your AGI exceeds certain levels.

V. Deductions from Adjusted Gross Income (AGI)

Once you have calculated your Adjusted Gross Income, you are then able to subtract the greater of either (1) Total Itemized Deductions or (2) Standardized Deductions.

1. Total itemized deductions can be separated into Major itemized deductions and Miscellaneous itemized deductions. Check the IRS website for further detail on itemized deductions especially given the changes to these deductions brought about by the Tax Cuts and Jobs Act of 2017.

    – Major itemized deductions include certain Medical expenses, Taxes, Interest, Charitable contributions and Casualty losses. The Tax Cuts and Jobs Act of 2017 capped the value of certain deductions at $10,000 starting in 2018. Please consult a tax professional regarding this and other changes.

    – Miscellaneous itemized deductions not subject to a 2% AGI floor include: Impairment-related work expenses, Gambling losses, but only to the extent of net winnings, annuity contract basis recovery, pro-rata portion of estate taxes paid due to income received in respect of decedent.

    – Miscellaneous itemized deductions subject to a 2% AGI floor include: employee business expenses, home office expenses, investment expenses, tax return preparation fees.

2. The Basic Standard Deductions are outlined below. In addition to these deductions, if you qualify you may take certain additional deductions if you are over 65 years of age and/or blind. The Tax Cuts and Jobs Act of 2017 combines the standard deduction and personal exemption in 2018

(essentially eliminating personal exemptions and increasing standard deductions). The 2017 and 2018 standard deduction levels are shown below.

Standard Deductions for 2017

Filing Status	Amount
Single	$6,350
Married Filing Jointly	$12,700
Qualifying Widower	$12,700
Head of Household	$9,350
Married Filing Seperately	$6,350

Source: Internal Revenue Service.

Standard Deductions for 2018

Filing Status	Amount
Single	$12,000
Married Filing Jointly	$24,000
Qualifying Widower	$24,000
Head of Household	$18,000
Married Filing Seperately	$12,000

Source: Internal Revenue Service.

VI. Personal and Dependency exemptions

When calculating your federal income tax, personal and dependency exemptions are deducted prior to reaching your taxable income. Your taxable income is the value to which your tax rate will then be applied. All of the below applies to the year 2017, but the Tax Cuts and Jobs Act of 2017 combines the standard deduction and personal exemption in 2018 (eliminating the exemptions that follow).

- An Individual can claim a $4,050 exemption for himself in 2017 and claim an additional $4,050 exemption for a spouse if they file a joint tax return.

- The tax code provides dependency exemptions for each qualifying child or qualifying relative of the taxpayer. A child may not have reached age

246

19, unless they are a student, in which case they can be 24 to be claimed as a dependent. A child can't qualify as a dependent on more than one tax return.

- Personal and dependency exemptions are subject to phase-outs based on AGI levels. Exemptions are reduced by 2% for a specific dollar amount above the specific thresholds.

VII. Taxable Income

After calculating your taxable income, you can apply tax credits that reduce the amount of your taxable income dollar for dollar. For further detail on these credits please check the IRS website. These tax credits include:

- Earned Income credit
- Credit for the elderly or disabled
- Foreign tax credit
- Child and dependent care credit
- Adoption credit
- Child tax credit (the Tax Cuts and Jobs Act of 2017 expanded the child tax credit to $2,000 starting in 2018)
- American Opportunity and Lifetime Learning Credit for education

How can taxes impact my investment portfolio and financial plan?

Taxes can bring down the value of your investment portfolio. Although we provide you some guidance, the taxation of investment income and various investment accounts can be extremely complex so if you have questions, contact a tax professional.

Individual Stocks: Stocks generate income for you through dividends and the appreciation of the stock's value. Dividends are taxed at two different rates (i) ordinary income rates for non-qualified dividends and (ii) lower capital gains tax rates for qualified dividends. Qualified dividends must meet IRS holding period requirements. Common stock held more than 60 days during the 121 day period beginning 60 days before the ex-dividend date are considered qualified. When you sell stock, it generates a capital gain. Capital gains are considered long-term for investments held 12 months or more, or short-term for investments held less than 12 months. Long-term gains are taxed at the more advantageous capital gains tax rate and short-term gains are taxed at your ordinary income rate.

Bonds: Bonds most often realize gains in the form of interest, but may also have capital gains. The interest is taxed at your ordinary income tax rate and capital gains are taxed at either your ordinary income rate if the holding period is short-term or the more advantageous capital gains tax rate if the holding period is long-term. The interest from Municipal bonds are not subject to federal income tax, and may avoid state taxes depending on your residency. Municipal bonds can generate capital gains, which would be taxed at your ordinary income tax rate if the gains are short-term and the capital gains tax rate if the gains are long-term.

Mutual Funds: If you hold a mutual fund in a taxable account, there are a number of ways you may be subject to tax. Mutual funds make distributions to shareholders on a regular basis regardless of if the shareholder desires them. The mutual fund will distribute ordinary interest and income generated by the underlying holdings in the fund. Interest income will be subject to ordinary income taxes. If dividends distributed by a mutual fund are qualified, they will be subject to a lower capital gains tax rate. If you sell a mutual fund the rate of tax you pay will depend on if the holding period is short-term (ordinary income tax) or long-term (capital gains tax). If you are going to purchase a mutual fund, try to make sure the turnover of the investments in the fund is low and that you do not buy a fund towards the end of the year when you are more likely to receive the full brunt of taxation without the benefits of a full year of ownership.

Exchange Traded Fund: In addition to lower expense fees, most ETFs are more tax efficient than mutual funds. Since ETFs follow an index, they experience less turnover of the underlying securities than actively managed mutual funds. In general, if you hold an ETF for more than 60 days, any dividends you receive will be qualified and you will pay a lower capital gains tax rate on these dividends. If you sell an ETF after holding it for one year or less, any gains will be subject to your ordinary income tax rate. If the ETF has been held for one year or more before a sale, any gains will be taxed at the more advantageous capital gains rate.

What is asset class "tax location"?

The location of your assets (the accounts they are held in) can help to reduce your tax bill. You will pay tax on all income and gains on investments you own in a taxable account (Individual, Joint, Transfer on Death). In a tax-deferred account such as an Individual Retirement Account (IRA), 401(k), Keogh or 403(b) you will only be subject to tax when you withdraw money from the account, allowing the assets to grow for long periods without incurring any tax. Roth IRAs are actually tax-free accounts that allow for tax-fee growth and tax-free withdrawal of your money once the account has been funded with after-tax assets.

Some investments are less tax-efficient than others. When possible, investments that distribute a high level of taxable income should be placed in a tax-deferred or a tax-free account. More tax-advantageous investments with lower taxed dividend distributions and long-term capital gains should be placed in taxable accounts. An example of the less tax-advantageous investments you should place in tax-deferred or tax-free accounts include:

- Corporate bonds and corporate bond funds
- Certificates of Deposit, agency bonds and mortgage bonds
- Mutual funds with high turnover of the underlying securities
- REITs and REIT mutual funds
- Commodity funds

An example of the more tax-advantageous investments you should generally place in taxable accounts include:

- Low turnover equity funds
- Broad market ETFs
- Municipal bonds and Municipal bond funds

Occasionally you will incur losses in a taxable account. You can use such losses to your advantage by offsetting taxable gains you may have in your investment accounts. Be sure when offsetting gains and losses, you match up short-term and long-term gains and losses. If there are losses that remain after offsetting all gains in a portfolio during a taxable year, up to $3,000 of these excess losses can be used to offset your ordinary income, lowering your tax bill. Any remaining losses at that point can be carried forward indefinitely.

Even if you don't need to raise cash by selling the security that has incurred the loss, you can still execute what is called a "tax swap". In a tax swap you sell the security with a loss, and then repurchase a similar, but not identical security to replace the security you sold. In this way you maintain your desired investment strategy but are able to take advantage of your loss.

Quick Tip: a more detailed explanation of tax swapping and the wash sale rule can be found here http://www.investopedia.com/terms/w/washsalerule.asp.

Glossary

401(k) Retirement Plans – a 401(k) is a qualified profit-sharing retirement savings plan sponsored by an employer. It lets you as an employee deduct savings from your paycheck before taxes are taken out. Taxes then aren't paid until the money is withdrawn from the 401 (k) account. You control how your money is invested. Most plans offer an array of funds composed of stocks, bonds, and money market investments. In most cases, you can't tap into your employer's contributions immediately. Vesting is the amount of time you must work for your company before gaining access to the company's payments into your 401(k). Your payments, on the other hand, vest immediately. On top of that, there are complex rules about when you can withdraw your money and costly penalties for pulling funds out before retirement age. You should invest enough to get the full matching amount that your company pays into the 401(k) plan. The IRS mandates contribution limits for 401(k) accounts. For 2018, the most you as a participant can put into your 401(k) is $18,500 in any combination of pre- and after-tax dollars. If you're older than 50, you can put in another $6,000. The total dollar amount that can be contributed including both your contributions and your employers contributions can't exceed the lesser of 100% of your salary or $55,000 in 2018.

529 Investment Program – a tax-advantaged investment vehicle in the United States designed to encourage saving for future higher education expenses of a designated beneficiary. 529 plans are named after section 529 of the Internal Revenue Code 26 U.S.C. § 529. Most states offer their own 529s. Many plans allow investors from out of state, but there can be significant advantages for those who invest in 529 plans in their state of residence. Contributions to a 529 grow tax-deferred and can be withdrawn free of tax if they are used for qualified higher education expenses.

Active Management – an investment strategy that seeks to outperform the average returns of the financial markets. Active managers rely on research, market forecasts and their own judgment or experience in selecting securities to buy and sell.

Adjusted Gross Income (AGI) – in the United States income tax system, as detailed on your IRS Form 1040, adjusted gross income (AGI) is your total gross income minus specific deductions. You can access these specific deductions on the IRS website.

American Opportunity Tax Credit – tax credit that helps students and parents to pay for part of their college expenses by providing a maximum annual tax credit per student of $2,500 towards the cost of qualified tuition and related expenses for the taxpayer, spouse or dependent. The student must be enrolled no less than part-time and the credit can be used no more than four times per student.

Assisted Living Facility – the greatest difference between an assisted living facility and an independent senior living is the care provided. Residents of assisted living facilities require assistance with daily activities like medication, eating, bathing, dressing, and toileting. Elderly people who have chosen to live in an assisted retirement complex will often require more care and support to improve their quality of life.

Beneficiary – a person or organization entitled to receive proceeds outlined in a legal document such as a will, trust, pay-on-death account or retirement plan. Generally, beneficiaries of wills receive their benefits only after the will is examined and approved by the probate court. Beneficiaries of living trusts receive their benefits outside of probate, as provided in the document establishing the trust. Retirement plan beneficiaries receive the proceeds of the account after the original account owner passes away. A primary beneficiary is a person who directly will benefit from a will or trust. A contingent beneficiary may or may not become a beneficiary depending on what happens to the primary beneficiary.

Beta – a measure of the magnitude of an investment security or portfolio's past share-price fluctuations in relation to the ups and downs of the overall market. The market is assigned a Beta of 1.0. This means if a security or portfolio has a Beta of 1.2 the security or portfolio will fall by 12% if the market falls 10%.

Cafeteria Benefit Plan – a type of employee benefit plan offered in the United States pursuant to Section 125 of the Internal Revenue Code. Allows employees to contribute a certain amount of their gross income to a designated account or accounts before this income is taxed. These accounts can be for insurance premiums and medical or dependent care expenses not covered by insurance, from which employees can be reimbursed throughout the plan year or claim period as they incur the expenses. A Cafeteria Plan allows an employer to reduce an employee's gross income, thereby reducing the amount the company pays in Federal Insurance Contributions Act (FICA or Social Security), Federal Unemployment Tax Act (FUTA), Workers' Compensation, and some State taxes.

Capital Gains Taxes – tax on the profit realized on the sale of a non-inventory asset that was purchased at a cost that was lower than the amount realized on the sale. If you hold your assets (stocks, bonds, securities) for longer than a year, you can benefit from the reduced capital gains tax rate on your profits. Short-term capital gains do not benefit from any special tax rate, they are taxed at the same rate as your ordinary income.

Cash Balance Plan – a defined benefit plan (as opposed to a defined contribution plan) with the same elevated contribution limits (the lesser of 100% of a participant's compensation averaged over the 3 highest years or a specified dollar amount), but it maintains hypothetical individual participant accounts and only the promise of a future benefit in the same manner as a defined contribution plan. In a typical Cash Balance Plan, each year a participant's account receives a "pay credit" based on compensation level and an "interest credit" representing returns on the participant's account. Often, this "interest credit" is tied to the Treasury Bill rate and amounts to a guaranteed market rate. The participant does not invest their own money, so the employer is still responsible for account performance. The benefit in a Cash Balance Pension plan is based on a set percentage of each participant's current annual salary and unlike a defined benefit plan does not consider how long the participant has been at the employer or future increases in salary. This means future benefits are more transparent, making Cash Balance Pension plans easier to fund than traditional defined benefit plans.

Charitable Trust – any trust designed to make a substantial gift to charity and also achieve income and estate tax savings for the grantor.

Coinsurance – amount you may be required to pay for health care services after you meet your plan's deductibles. In Medicare Part A and Part B, this is a percentage (usually 20%) of the Medicare-approved amount. You have to pay this amount after you pay the deductible for Medicare Part A and/or Medicare Part B. In a Medicare Prescription Drug Plan (Part D), the coinsurance will vary depending on how much you have spent.

Community Property – a system of marital property ownership followed by a handful of states under which, in general, all property acquired after marriage and before any sort of permanent separation is considered to belong equally to both spouses. Property that is gifted or inherited is not subject to this and is owned by the spouse that received it.

Consolidated Omnibus Budget Reconciliation Act of 1985 (COBRA) – used for the purposes of extending an individual's healthcare coverage, the key part of COBRA implements an excise (penalty) tax on employers (generally with 20 or more employees) if they do not offer an extension of an employee's healthcare plan once a "qualifying event" occurs. Qualifying events include (i) death of the covered employee (ii) an employee loses eligibility for coverage due to a reduction in hours (iii) divorce or legal separation that terminates an ex-spouses coverage and (iv) a dependent child reaching the age they are no longer covered.

Coupon Rate – in an investment portfolio, the interest rate a bond issuer promises to pay the bondholder until the bond matures.

Coverage Gap - Medicare Part D – period of time in which you pay higher cost share for prescription drugs, until you spend enough to qualify for catastrophic coverage. The coverage gap (also called the "donut hole") starts when you and your plan have paid a set dollar amount for prescription drugs during that year. During this coverage gap period in Medicare Part D (prescription drug coverage), your drug costs may increase.

Coverdell Education Savings Account – a tax-deferred trust account created by the U.S. government to assist families in funding educational expenses for beneficiaries 18 years old or younger. While more than one Coverdell can be set up for a single beneficiary, the total maximum contribution per year for any single beneficiary is $2,000. Distributions are tax-free if the distributions aren't more than the beneficiary's adjusted qualified education expenses for the year.

Credit Rating – pertains to the fixed income portion of an investment portfolio. A published ranking based on careful financial analysis of a creditor's ability to pay the interest and principal owed on the debt. The possibility that a bond issuer will fail to repay interest and principal in a timely manner is called credit or default risk. You can see a breakdown of fixed income credit ratings at https://www.fidelity.com/learning-center/investment-products/fixed-income-bonds/bond-ratings.

Custodian – a person named to care for property left to a minor under the Uniform Transfer to Minor Act (UTMA) or the Uniform Gift to Minors Act (UGMA). In addition, the company that services an IRA or other account may be referred to as a custodian.

DB(k) plan – a "hybrid" plan designed to address the potential shortfalls in Section 401(k) plans and the decline in establishing defined benefit plans. Starting in 2010, traditional defined benefit plans could start accepting 401(k)-type pre-tax employee contributions. The employer implementing a DB(k) plan can't have more than 500 employees. As part of a DB(k) plan, the Section 401(k) component must include an automatic enrollment feature. This automatic enrollment feature, typically results in greater participant savings. A DB(k) plan must allow for a fully vested 50% employer match on the first 4% deferred by the employee. This type of plan combines the monthly income and security at retirement a participant receives in a defined benefit plan with the individual investment control found in defined contribution plans.

Defined Benefit Pension Plan – a type of pension plan in which an employer/sponsor promises a specified monthly benefit upon retirement that is predetermined by a formula based on the employee's earnings history, tenure of service and age, rather than depending directly on individual investment returns. Investment risk and portfolio management are entirely under the control of the company. There are also restrictions on when and how you can withdraw these funds without penalties.

Dividend Yield – in an investment portfolio, the annual rate of return on a security, determined by dividing the annual dividend by the current share price.

Dollar Cost Averaging – investing equal amounts of money at regular intervals on an ongoing basis. The technique ensures that investor buys fewer shares when prices are high and more shares when prices are low. A 401(k) with regular deferrals and contributions naturally accomplishes this.

Durable Power of Attorney – power of attorney that remains effective even if the person who created it (called the "principal") becomes incapacitated. The person authorized to act (the "attorney-in-fact") can make health care decisions and handle financial affairs for the principal.

Social Security Earnings test – the retirement earnings test may limit the Social Security benefits you are able to receive prior to your full retirement age (FRA) dependent on the amount you earn. Social Security withholds benefits if your earnings exceed one of two different levels.

Earnings per Share – the portion of a company's profit allocated to each outstanding share of common stock. Earnings per share serves as an indicator of a company's profitability.

Effective Tax Rate – the average rate at which your earned income is taxed. Your effective tax rate is calculated by dividing total tax expense by taxable income. Note that your effective tax rate is lower than your marginal tax rate which is the tax rate you pay on an incremental dollar of income.

Employee Stock Ownership Plan (ESOP) – an ESOP borrows funds from a lending institution such as a bank to purchase employer stock. The employer then distributes this stock to ESOP participants and continues to pay off the loan through tax-deductible contributions to the ESOP. The employer is limited to a deduction equivalent to 25% of covered compensation, unless the excess is attributable to loan interest, which is deductible regardless of percentage of covered compensation. An ESOP creates a broader market and improves liquidity for employer stock. An employer offering an ESOP must provide plan participants an opportunity to sell back stock to the employer (a put option) during a 60 day period immediately following distribution and again for 60 days during the following plan year. Stock bonus plans and ESOPs can be particularly complex so you should consult a trusted advisor, particularly when taking distributions from these plans. Shareholders can realize tax benefits by selling shares to an ESOP in the form of deferred capital gains as long as proceeds from the sale are reinvested in domestic securities. This tax benefit is only available if (i) the ESOP owns at least 30% of employer stock (ii) shareholder held the stock for at least three years and (iii) qualified replacement property must be purchased within one year after the sale.

Exchange Traded Fund (ETF) – an ETF, or exchange traded fund, is a marketable security that tracks an index, a commodity, bonds, or a basket of assets like an index fund. Unlike mutual funds, an ETF trades like a common stock on a stock exchange. ETFs experience price changes throughout the day as they are bought and sold. ETFs typically have higher daily liquidity and lower fees than mutual fund shares, making them an attractive alternative for individual investors.

Executor – the person named in your will to manage your estate, deal with the probate court, collect your assets, and distribute them as you specified. If you die without a will, the probate court will appoint an "administrator" for your estate.

Expected Family Contribution – a term used in the college financial aid process to determine an applicant's eligibility for need-based federal student aid, and in many cases, state and institutional aid. Your Expected Family Contribution is provided on the Student Aid Report (SAR) and Institutional Student Information Record (ISIR) sent to you after the FAFSA is processed. This is an estimate of the parents and/or student's ability to contribute to post-secondary education expenses.

Expense Ratio – the percentage of a portfolio's average net assets used to pay its annual expenses. The expense ratio, can include management fees, administrative fees and any 12b-1 fees. All of these expenses directly detract from the returns of a portfolio. Gross returns do not include fees, while net returns include a deduction for fees.

Equivalent Taxable Yield – when examining fixed income investments, the yield needed from a taxable bond to give the same after-tax yield as a tax-exempt issue (Municipal bond).

Federal Application for Federal Student Aid (FAFSA) – a form that can be prepared annually by current and prospective college students (undergraduate and graduate) in the United States to determine their eligibility for student financial aid. In addition to demographic and financial information, applicants are asked to list up to ten schools to receive the results of the application once it is processed. Need-based aid has to be reapplied for each year. You can access and fill out the FAFSA form at studentaid.ed.gov.

Federal Pell Grant – when funding college costs, unlike a loan, does not have to be repaid. Federal Pell Grants usually are awarded only to undergraduate students who have not earned a bachelor's or a professional degree. Amounts can change yearly. The amount you receive will depend on need and cost of college attendance.

Federal Perkins Loan Program – Perkins Loans, are low-interest federal student loans for undergraduate and graduate students with exceptional financial need.

Federal PLUS Loans – federal loans that graduate or professional degree students and parents of dependent undergraduate students can use to help pay education expenses. The maximum amount that can be borrowed is based on the cost of college attendance less any aid received, effectively allowing you to cover all remaining college expenses once other funding resources have been used.

Federal Reserve – the Central Bank that regulates the supply of money and credit throughout the United States. The Federal Reserve's seven-member board of governors is appointed by the president and has significant influence on U.S. monetary and fiscal economic policy. The Federal Reserve's direct influence on interest rates is one of its key and most widely known financial functions.

Federal Stafford Loans – Stafford Loans are available both as subsidized and unsubsidized loans. Subsidized loans are offered to students based on demonstrated financial need and the interest on subsidized loans is paid by the federal government while the student is in school during authorized deferment periods. Unsubsidized Stafford Loans are not dependent on need and you are responsible for all of the interest that accrues while the student is enrolled in school.

Federal Supplemental Educational Opportunity Grant (FSEOG) – to get an FSEOG, you must fill out the FAFSA so your college can determine how much financial need you have. Students who will receive Federal Pell Grants and have the most financial need will receive the FSEOG first.

Flexible Spending Account (FSA) – special account you put money into that is used to pay for certain out-of-pocket health care costs. You don't have to pay income taxes on this money. This means you'll save an amount equal to the taxes you would have paid on the money you set aside in the FSA. You can use funds in your FSA to pay for certain medical and dental expenses, including copayments and deductibles. FSAs are available only with employment-based health plans. Employers may make contributions to your FSA. You can't spend FSA funds on insurance premiums. You can put up to $2,650 into an FSA each year and generally must use that money within the plan year.

Full Retirement Age – Social Security's full retirement age (FRA) increases gradually because of legislation passed in 1983 to raise its level. The FRA is 65 for those born prior to 1943. The FRA is 66 for those born from 1943 – 1954 and will gradually rise to age 67 for those born 1960 or later. Your FRA is a key social security variable because if you collect benefits below this age your benefits will be reduced and if you delay retirement past this age your benefits will rise.

Geriatric Care Manager – professionals who can assess older adult care requirements and develop a plan that will examine the need for in-home care, relocation, additional medical care as well as the coordination of all related services. Geriatric Care Managers can be the eyes and ears for family members who live far away or nearby, but are too busy to handle the daily details of the older person's life.

Government Pension Offset – when it comes to Social Security, if you receive a pension from a federal, state, or local government based on work for which you didn't pay Social Security taxes, the Social Security administration may reduce your Social Security, spouses or widows/widowers benefits.

Gross Income – gross income includes "all income from whatever source", and is not limited to cash received. It specifically includes wages, salary, bonuses, interest, dividends, rents, royalties, income from operating a business, alimony, pensions and annuities, share of income from partnerships and S corporations, and income tax refunds.

Health Care Directive (Living Will) – a document in which you state your wishes regarding health care in case you are ever unable to speak and/or name a trusted person to see that your wishes are carried out.

Health Maintenance Organization (HMO) – a managed health care plan that generally offers coverage of the services provided within the HMO plan's network. Medicare members may get their benefits through an HMO. This includes a Medicare Advantage (Medicare Part C) plan with coverage for Medicare Part A and Part B. HMO beneficiaries must choose a primary care physician (PCP) to act as a coordinator and "gatekeeper" to their health care.

Health Savings Account (HSA) – is a tax-advantaged medical savings account available to taxpayers in the United States who are enrolled in a high-deductible health plan (HDHP). An HSA gives you a triple tax break: Your contributions are sheltered from income taxes, the money grows tax-deferred, and the funds can be withdrawn tax-free for medical expenses. Unlike a flexible spending account (FSA), HSA funds roll over and accumulate year to year if not spent. HSAs are owned by the individual, which differentiates them from company-owned Health Reimbursement Arrangements (HRA) which act as an alternate tax-deductible source of funds paired with either HDHPs or standard health plans.

Home Health Care – aide services and skilled nursing care provided within the confines of your home, on a limited part-time basis. The care may include occupational therapy, physical therapy, medical social services, speech-language pathology services, durable medical equipment (such as hospital beds, oxygen, wheelchairs, and walkers), medical supplies, and other services.

Hospice Care – care provided for people who are terminally ill. It includes inpatient care and outpatient care, counseling, pain management, respite care, prescription drugs, as well as services for the person's family or caregiver. Hospice care is covered under Medicare Part A (hospital insurance).

Independent Living Facility – facility typically has no personal or healthcare services. You rent or purchase an apartment or smaller home in an independent living community. Independent senior living facilities do not provide health care, 24/7 skilled nursing or assistance with activities of daily living (ADLs).

Individual Retirement Account (IRA) – an IRA is a non-qualified, tax-advantaged retirement plan set up at a financial institution that allows you to save for retirement with tax-free growth of your investments. An IRA can help supplement your current savings in your employer-sponsored retirement plan. Through an IRA you can gain access to a wider variety of lower-cost investment options than an employer's 401(k). There are three main types of IRAs—Traditional, Roth, and Rollover—each with different advantages. In a Traditional IRA, you make contributions with money you may be able to deduct on your tax return and any earnings can potentially grow tax-deferred until you withdraw them in retirement. Many retirees also find themselves in a lower tax bracket than they were in pre-retirement, so the tax-deferral means the money may be taxed at a lower rate. With a Roth IRA, you make contributions with money you've already paid taxes on (after-tax) and your money may potentially grow tax-free, with tax-free withdrawals in retirement, provided certain conditions are met. A Rollover IRA is a Traditional IRA intended for money that is "rolled over" from a qualified retirement plan. Rollovers involve moving eligible assets from an employer-sponsored plan, such as a 401(k) or 403(b), into an IRA.

Inflation Risk – the possibility that increases in cost of living will reduce or eliminate the returns on a particular investment. This is especially a concern for bond investments because they provide investors with a fixed stream of income.

Inpatient and Outpatient Hospital Care – inpatient health care services are provided in a hospital or skilled nursing facility. Outpatient hospital care is medical or surgical care that does not require you to stay in a hospital overnight.

Interest Rate Risk – for fixed income investments, the possibility that a security or mutual fund will decline in value because of an increase in interest rates. This is particularly a concern for bond investments that provide investors with a fixed stream of income. Previously issued bonds become less valuable when similar investments are issued that pay a higher rate of return.

Investment Grade Bonds – a bond whose credit quality is considered to be among the highest by independent bond-rating agencies. Due to the high credit quality, investors can expect less volatility, but lower returns from these bonds.

IRS Form 1040 – the IRS Form 1040 is one of the official documents that you as a taxpayer can use to file your annual income tax return. The form is divided into sections where you can report your income and deductions to determine the amount of tax you owe or the refund you can expect to receive. Depending on the type of income you report, it may be necessary to attach other forms or schedules to it.

Itemized Deductions – as a taxpayer you are allowed a choice between itemized deductions and the standard deduction. After computing your adjusted gross income (AGI), you can itemize your deductions (from a list of allowable items) and subtract those itemized deductions from your AGI to arrive at your taxable income. As a taxpayer you may deduct the total itemized deduction amount, or the standard deduction amount, whichever is greater. You can access a full list of itemized deductions on the IRS website.

Joint Tenancy – a way to take title to jointly owned real or personal property. When two or more people own property as joint tenants, and one of the owners dies, the other owner(s) of the property automatically become owners of the deceased owners share. A joint tenancy interest does not go through probate.

Junk Bond – in fixed income investing, a bond with a credit rating of BB or lower. Known as "High-Yield" bonds, these bonds are subject to greater price volatility and credit risk than other types of bonds because of the lower quality of the underlying companies issuing them. There are greater returns available to those willing to take on the additional risk of these lower-quality bonds

Lifetime Learning Credit – a provision of the U.S. federal income tax code that lets parents and students lower their tax liability by up to $2,000 to help offset higher education expenses. The Lifetime Learning Credit matches dollar for dollar, up to the $2,000 limit, the amount that the parent or student spends on qualified education expenses for a student enrolled at an eligible post-secondary educational institution. A 20% factor applies to a maximum of $10,000 of qualified expenses. There is no limit on the number of years you can take the Lifetime Learning Credit, but it cannot be combined with the American Opportunity Credit in the same tax year.

Living Trust – a trust set up while a person is alive and that remains under the control of the person until death. Often referred to as "inter vivos trust". An excellent way to minimize the value of property passing through probate. This is because it enables the person creating the trust (grantor) to specify that money or other property will pass directly to their beneficiaries at the time of death free of probate. Note that during life, depending on the terms the grantor can often control property, change beneficiaries or even end the trust.

Long-term care – a variety of services which help meet both the medical and non-medical needs of people with a chronic illness or disability who cannot care for themselves for long periods of time. It is common for long-term care to provide custodial and non-skilled care, such as assisting with normal daily tasks like dressing, feeding, or using the bathroom. Long-term care can involve providing a level of medical care that requires the expertise of skilled practitioners to address the multiple chronic conditions associated with older populations. Long-term care can be provided at home, in assisted living facilities or in nursing homes.

Long-term Capital Gain – a profit on the sale of a security or mutual fund share that has been held for more than one year. When sold, these securities are generally subject to the lower capital gains tax rate as opposed to the more elevated ordinary income tax rate.

Long-term care insurance – individuals who require long-term care are generally not sick in the traditional sense, but instead, are unable to perform the basic activities of daily living (ADLs) such as dressing, bathing, eating, toileting, continence, transferring (getting in and out of a bed or chair), and walking. Long-term care insurance generally covers home care, assisted living, adult daycare, respite care, hospice care, nursing home and Alzheimer's facilities. Long-term care insurance can pay for home care, often from the first day it is needed. In addition, it will pay for a visiting or live-in caregiver, companion, housekeeper, therapist or private duty nurse up to seven days a week, 24 hours a day (up to the policy benefit maximum).

Marginal Tax Rate – the amount of tax you would pay on an additional dollar of income. Your marginal tax rate will increase as income rises. This method of taxation aims to fairly tax individuals based upon their earnings, with low income earners being taxed at a lower rate than higher income earners.

Marital Deduction – in estate taxation, an unlimited deduction (really more like an exemption) allowed by federal estate tax law for all property passed to a surviving spouse.

Medicare – a social insurance program, administered by the federal government, that also uses private insurance companies. Medicare provides health insurance for Americans aged 65 and older who have worked and paid Medicare taxes in the past. It also provides health insurance to younger people with disabilities, end stage renal disease and amyotrophic lateral sclerosis (ALS). Medicare consists of four parts, Medicare Part A (hospital insurance), Medicare Part B (medical insurance), Medicare Part C (Medicare Advantage Plans) and Medicare Part D (prescription drug coverage).

Medicare Part A – in general Medicare Part A covers inpatient hospital care (inpatient simply means your services occur within the hospital), home health services, skilled nursing facility care, and hospice care. Most people are automatically eligible for Medicare Part A at age 65 if they have worked at least 10 years (40 quarters) and paid Medicare taxes during that time. If you do not qualify based on your work credits you can pay a premium to enroll as well. You may also qualify for Medicare Part A if you have a disability, end-stage renal disease or amyotrophic lateral sclerosis.

Medicare Part B – medical insurance that covers certain non-hospital expenses like doctor's office visits, blood tests, medical supplies and outpatient hospital care. Medicare Part B requires a monthly premium that may be higher depending on your income. You are typically responsible for a portion of your Medicare Part B costs. You must pay a deductible before benefits kick in and then very likely will have to cover 20% of qualified expenses. If the doctor or service provider does not accept Medicare Part B you may be responsible for the total bill.

Medicare Part C – also known as Medicare Advantage, is insurance that often covers every type of Medicare coverage in one health plan. Medicare Advantage Plans are required to provide all Medicare Part A and Medicare Part B benefits, but Medicare Advantage Plans may include a variety of additional benefits as well. The government contracts with private insurance companies that then offer Medicare Advantage Plans to consumers. Technically you must have Medicare Part A and Medicare Part B (while continuing to pay your Part B premium) to enroll in a Medicare Advantage Plan.

Medicare Part D – provides optional prescription drug coverage. Medicare Part D is available through private insurance companies as a stand-alone prescription drug plan. In addition, you can get prescription drug coverage through a Medicare Advantage Prescription Drug plan if there is one offered in your geographical area. You will share in the cost of your prescription drugs either through a deductible, a flat co-payment, or co-insurance.

Medigap Supplemental Plan – as an alternative to Medicare Part C, Medigap helps to cover the "gap" between what you pay out-of-pocket and what you pay under Medicare Part A and Medicare Part B. You can get this type of Medicare Supplement policy through private insurance companies. There are 10 different policies to choose from. Medigap policies are regulated by state and federal law so all coverage options are the same, with the difference being price and who administers the plan.

Money Purchase Pension Plan (MPP) – is a defined contribution plan and not a defined benefit plan, so it has total contribution limits of the lesser of $55,000 or 100% of the participant's salary. Like other pension plans though, it requires mandatory annual contributions to each participant's account based on a formula. The employer incurs an excise tax if they do not make required minimum annual contributions. Plan participants are responsible for investment performance. The formula is non-discriminatory and either a fixed percentage or dollar amount of the participant's salary. This makes an MPP simpler to define, fund and administer than a traditional defined benefit plan. In addition, an MPP does not require actuarial work or PBGC insurance, making it less expensive than a traditional defined benefit plan.

Municipal Bond Fund – tax-exempt bonds issued by state, city, and/or local governments. The interest payments for this type of bond are not subject to federal taxation and in some cases are not subject to state or local taxes.

Net Worth Statement – a personal Net Worth Statement is a snapshot of your financial health, at one particular point in time. It is a summary of what you own (assets) less what is owed to others (liabilities). The overall formula for your Net Worth Statement is [assets – liabilities = net worth]. If your assets are greater than your liabilities, you have a positive net worth. If your assets are less than your liabilities you have a negative net worth.

Nursing Home Facility – a place of residence for people who require continual nursing care and have significant difficulty coping with the required activities of daily living. Nursing aides and skilled nurses are usually available 24 hours a day.

Passive Management – a style of management where a fund's portfolio mirrors a market index. Followers of passive management believe in the efficient market hypothesis which states that at all times markets incorporate and reflect all information, rendering individual stock picking futile. As a result, the best investing strategy is to invest in index funds, which, historically, have outperformed the majority of actively managed funds.

Pay-on-death (P.O.D.) designation – a method of providing, on a property account form, who will inherit what remains of your property when you die. This is most commonly used for bank accounts as a way to avoid probate.

Preferred Provider Organization (PPO Plan) – a type of Medicare Advantage (Medicare Part C) in which you must use providers in the plan's network. You can also receive partial coverage of care from out-of-network providers as part of this type of plan, but may pay more for these services. People with Medicare can choose to get their Medicare benefits through a PPO.

Price/Earning (P/E) Ratio – the share price of a stock divided by its per-share earnings over the past year. The P/E ratio can be a good indicator of market expectations about a company's prospects. The higher the P/E ratio, the greater the expectations for a company's future earnings growth. Be wary though of a company's ability to manipulate their bottom line earnings number.

Primary Insurance Amount – these are the Social Security retirement benefits a person will receive upon reaching his or her full retirement age (FRA). If you elect to receive Social Security prior to this age, your full benefits will be reduced. If you elect to receive Social Security past FRA your Social Security benefits will rise.

Private fee-for-service Plan – a type of Medicare Advantage (Medicare Part C) plan in which you may go to any Medicare-approved doctor, hospital, or any other health care provider that accepts the plan's payment. The Private Fee-for-Service Plan (rather than Medicare) will make decisions on how much it will pay and how much you will pay for the services you get. You may have extra benefits that original Medicare Part A and Part B doesn't cover, and you may pay more or less for Medicare-covered benefits under this type of plan.

Probate – court proceeding in which (i) the authenticity of your will is established (ii) your executor or administrator is appointed (iii) your debts and taxes are paid

(iv) your heirs are identified and (v) the property in your probate estate is distributed according to your will.

Provisional Income – used in calculating the amount of tax that may potentially be applied to your Social Security benefits if you have reached your full retirement age. Your provisional income is your Modified Adjusted Gross Income (MAGI) plus one half of the Social Security benefit you receive. Your MAGI is defined as your taxable income (Adjusted Gross Income) plus non-taxable items such as student loan interest, adoption expenses etc.

Qualified Domestic Trust (QDOT) – a trust used to postpone estate tax when a U.S. citizen wants to leave property to a non-U.S. citizen spouse because the unlimited marital deduction can't be applied to a non-U.S. citizen spouse.

Qualified Retirement Plan – established by your employer and described in Section 401(a) of the U.S. Tax Code. The adherence to Section 401(a) allows the qualified plan to utilize special tax advantages so that in general, your contributions are not taxed until you withdraw money from the qualified plan. The most common types of qualified plans can be categorized as profit sharing plans (including 401(k) plans) or pension plans (defined benefit plans). Under profit sharing plans, also referred to as defined contribution plans, the amount you will receive in your retirement is dependent on how well you manage your own investments. In contrast, your employer is responsible for investment performance and retirement payments as part of a pension plan.

Qualified Terminal Interest Property (QTIP) Trust – a marital trust with property or ongoing income left for the use of the surviving spouse during the course of their life (life beneficiary). No estate taxes are assessed on the property until the death of the second spouse.

Real Estate Investment Trust (REIT) – a company that manages a group of real estate investments and distributes at least 90 percent of its net earnings annually to stockholders. REITs often specialize in a particular type of property (office buildings, apartments, shopping centers and hotels). REITs can either purchase real estate (equity REIT) or provide loans to building developers (mortgage REIT).

Real Return – the actual return received on an investment after factoring in inflation. For example, if the nominal rate of return on a particular investment is 8% and inflation is 3%, the real return would be 5% (8% nominal – 3% inflation).

Required Beginning Date (RBD) – is the date by which retirement account owners must begin making distributions from their accounts. This date is April 1st of the calendar year after turning age 70½ or April 1st of the calendar year after retiring, whichever is later. If the retirement plan owner is a 5% owner of the business sponsoring the retirement plan, there is no option to take the distribution on April 1st of the calendar year after retiring.

Required Minimum Distribution (RMD) – retirement account owners must begin making distributions from their accounts by April 1st of the calendar year after turning age 70½ or April 1st of the calendar year after retiring, whichever is later. Although you have the option to take this distribution in April of the year you turn 70½, in that year as well as each year thereafter, you will take the distribution on December 31st. The value of these distributions is based on life expectancy according to the relevant factors from the appropriate IRS tables. There is an exception to minimum distribution for people still working once they reach 70½. The exception only applies to the current plan they are participating in and does not apply if the account owner is a 5% owner of the business sponsoring the retirement plan. A Roth IRA is not subject to minimum distribution rules. If you do not take your required minimum distribution, the IRS penalty is 50% of the amount that should have been distributed.

Retirement Plan Catch-up Contribution – employees that participate in a qualified plan who are 50 years old or over at any time during the year are allowed additional pre-tax "catch-up" of $6,000. The pre-tax "catch-up" allowances for other non-qualified retirement plans such as IRAs, SIMPLEs and SEPs vary from the catch-up for qualified plans.

Retirement Plan Rollover – if you change or leave a job, you do not necessarily have to take a distribution from the retirement plan you have with your former employer. If you did opt for a full distribution and are not yet 59½, you will have to pay ordinary income tax and a 10% penalty tax on the funds you take. You have a few other options aside from taking a full distribution of your retirement plan. These options include (i) keeping your money in your former employer's plan and (ii) rolling the money over into a new 401(k) plan or IRA. If you choose to keep your money in your former employer's plan, you have to have a fully vested total of at least $5,000 in your account, and you have to be under the plan's normal retirement age (usually 65). If you decide to roll over your funds into another 401(k) or IRA you must first contact your old employer to fill out the appropriate rollover paperwork. If you are rolling the funds into a new employers 401(k) work with your new employer to execute the roll over. If you are rolling the funds into an IRA, make sure to set up a new IRA if you do not have an existing IRA account. (iii) You can have the rollover check be written directly to you. If it does come to you rather than a new account (such as an IRA), you'll be charged the tax and the 10% penalty.

Roth IRA Rollover – you can transfer some or all of your existing balance in a traditional IRA to a Roth IRA, regardless of income. You can convert all or part of other retirement accounts, such as an employer-sponsored 401(k) or 403b plan, to a Roth IRA too. You can do this once you leave your job, or in some cases, even while you continue to work for the same employer. Some plans allow you to access the money while you are still working, known as an "in-service distribution", but you usually have to reach age 59 ½ before you can do so. When you move money from a pre-tax retirement account such as a traditional IRA or 401(k) to a Roth, you have to pay taxes on this amount. The amount being converted will be added to your current year's income and you will pay ordinary income tax.

Savings/Thrift plan (Thrift plan) – a qualified defined contribution plan that encourages after-tax contributions by participants through the offer of an employer match. Participant contributions to the plan are not tax deductible, but employer contributions and earnings on employer contributions grow tax deferred. As with most other contribution plans, the maximum elective deferral a participant can make into a Thrift plan is $18,500 annually with an additional $6,000 "catch-up" for participants 50 or older. An employer typically makes a matching contribution based on a predetermined formula. Thrift plans must meet the ACP test, but are not required to meet the ADP test because employee contributions are after-tax. Thrift plans are offered to U.S. civil service employees and retirees, as well as members of the uniformed services. Outside of this arena, Thrift plans have generally been replaced by 401(k) plans, but are often used as a supplement to other types of retirement plans.

Series EE Savings Bonds – among the most widely held forms of government debt, they have evolved over time and exist in several forms. Most often they are used to help pay for qualified higher education expenses or to satisfy other individual liabilities. Qualified higher education expenses include rolling over the funds from the Series EE or Series I Savings Bond into a qualified tuition program such as a 529 or a Coverdell ESA.

Short-term Capital Gain – a profit on the sale of a security or mutual fund share that has been held for one year or less. When sold, these securities are generally subject to the more elevated ordinary income tax rate as opposed to the lower capital gains tax rate.

Simplified Employee Pension IRA (SEP IRA) – a variation of the Individual Retirement Account (IRA). SEP IRAs are adopted by business owners to provide retirement benefits for the business owners and their employees. The deadline for establishing the plan and making contributions is the filing deadline for the employer's tax return, including extensions. The strictest conditions employers may place on employee eligibility are as follows (1) employee has attained age 21 (2) employee has worked for the employer in three of the previous five years (3) employee has received at least $600 in compensation for the tax year. SEP contributions can be as much as 25% of compensation with a maximum contribution of $55,000 per individual. Note employees can't make their own deferrals into a SEP IRA.

Simplified Incentive Match Plan for Employees (SIMPLE IRA) – a retirement plan that may be established by employers, including self-employed individuals. The SIMPLE IRA allows eligible employees to contribute part of their pre-tax compensation to the plan. This means the tax on the money is deferred until it is distributed. This contribution is called an elective-deferral or salary-reduction contribution. Employers are required to make either matching contributions, which are based only on elective-deferral contributions made by employees, or non-elective contributions, which are paid to each eligible employee regardless of whether the employee made salary-reduction contributions to the plan. For a matching contribution, the employer's contribution may match the employee's elective-deferral contribution dollar for dollar, up to a maximum of 3% of the employee's compensation. They must make matching contributions or non-elective contributions by the due date (including extensions) of their federal income tax return for the year. If an employer has no other retirement plans they may set up a SIMPLE if the employer employed 100 or fewer employees who earned at least $5,000 during the preceding year. The amount an employee contributes from their salary to a SIMPLE IRA cannot exceed $12,500.

Skilled Nursing Care – medically necessary care performed by a therapist or skilled nurse. Generally, includes care from a Registered Nurse and/or a Licensed Practical Nurse. This skilled nursing care most often follows serious illness, injury or surgery. It will require high levels of specialized care and last for a matter of days or weeks. Custodial care typically involves assistance with the tasks of daily living. Tasks of daily living include eating, dressing, bathing and moving around. This assistance most often occurs in a nursing home, but can occur in your own home as well.

Social Security Administration – an independent agency of the U.S. federal government that administers social insurance programs consisting of retirement, disability and survivor's benefits. To qualify for these benefits, you pay Social Security taxes on earnings during your lifetime. You can contact the Social Security Administration via their website at www.socialsecurity.gov or toll free at 1-800-772-1213. In addition, most cities have a local Social Security office you can visit in person. If you have not done so already that you sign up for a "my Social Security" account to access your current Social Security data.

Social Security Dependent Benefits – benefits provided to those that are married to a retired or disabled worker who qualified for Social Security retirement or disability benefits. The dependent and minor or disabled children may be entitled to benefits based on a spouse's earnings record.

Social Security Retirement Benefits – monthly benefits you receive when you retire. The size of your benefits is based on your 35 highest paid working years. You can take retirement benefits any time from age 62 to age 70. The older you are when you begin taking benefits, the higher your monthly payouts will be (see definition of Full Retirement Age).

Social Security Survivor Benefits – as the surviving spouse of a worker who qualified for Social Security benefits, you and your minor or disabled children may be entitled to benefits based on your deceased spouse's earnings record.

Split-Dollar Life Insurance Policy – an arrangement between an employer and an employee to share the costs and benefits of a life insurance policy. Specifically, the parties join together to purchase an insurance policy on the life of the employee and agree, in writing, to split the cost of the insurance premiums, as well as the policy's death proceeds, cash value, and other benefits. The actual life insurance policy used can be whole life, universal life, second-to-die (survivorship), or any other cash value policy. Split dollar arrangements usually take one of two forms. Under the endorsement form, the employer is formally designated as the owner of the life insurance contract and endorses the contract to specify the portion of the death proceeds payable to the employee's beneficiary. Under the collateral assignment form, the employee is formally designated as the owner of the contract, and the employer premium advances are secured by a collateral assignment of the policy.

Standard Deductions – as an alternative to subtracting itemized deductions, you can elect to subtract the standard deduction from your income based on your tax filing to arrive at your taxable income. A taxpayer may deduct the total itemized deduction amount, or the standard deduction amount, whichever is greater. You can access the value of the standard deductions you are able to take on the IRS website.

Stock Bonus Plan – benefits in an employer stock bonus plan are distributed in the form of employer stock as opposed to cash. A stock bonus plan may permit employee contributions, but typically does not. Like other profit-sharing plans, benefits can be determined in a variety of ways (such as a percentage of either profits or covered payroll). The annual additions to a participant's account are limited to the lesser of 100% of the employee's compensation or $55,000 with a "catch-up" contribution of $6,000 available for participants over 50. Taxation to the employee on employer contributions is deferred as with other qualified plans. Stock bonus plans are subject to the same non-discrimination requirements as traditional profit-sharing plans. Distributions are in the form of employer stock and if there is no established market, participants may have a put option requiring the employer to purchase participant stock. Upon a participant's retirement, disability or death, distributions must be made within one year. Other types of participant separation from an employer require distributions occur within 5 years. Lump-sum distributions of employer stock may allow a participant the ability to defer net unrealized appreciation (NUA) on employer securities and potentially pay a lower tax rate on gains.

Student Aid Report (SAR) – shows the federal government's conclusions about the student's eligibility for need-based financial aid, based on the FAFSA. The SAR shows the Expected Family Contribution, based on the information on the FAFSA, and lists which need-based aid the student is eligible for. The SAR should be carefully reviewed for errors. An electronic version of the SAR (called an ISIR) is made available to the colleges/universities the student selects on the FAFSA. The ISIR is also sent to state agencies that award need-based aid.

Target Benefit Plan – technically these are defined contribution plans because they involve fixed contributions which are independent of a plan's funded position. Annual funding is limited to the lesser of $55,000 or 100% of the participant's salary. Funding is actuarily determined based upon a target benefit and a contribution is then made to the participant's account each year. The actuarial formula is only determined in the participant's first year of enrollment and does not change thereafter (does not account for future salary increases). This makes funding much less difficult to predict than in a traditional defined benefit plan. Like a defined benefit plan, annual contributions are determined by formula, but like a defined contribution plan there is no guarantee of the benefit to be paid. Age is a key factor in the determination of benefits and older employees are favored in Target Benefit plans as they have less time to achieve the target benefit. Target Benefit plans were more popular historically when they offered employers larger deductions than other types of retirement plans, but this advantage has since ceased.

Tax-Advantaged Retirement Plans – are not technically qualified plans because they do not adhere to the rules outlined in Section 401(a) of the U.S. tax code, but have many similarities to qualified plans particularly when it comes to tax treatment. These tax-advantaged plans include Individual Retirement Accounts (IRAs) which you can open yourself, as well as 403(b) and 457(b) plans which cover employees of public schools, charities, state and local governments.

Tax Deferral – refers to instances where a taxpayer can delay paying taxes until some future period. The advantage to this is that you may be taxed at a lower rate in the future, particularly for deferral of income taxes.

Taxable Income – the amount of income that is used to calculate your income tax due. Taxable income is generally described as gross income or adjusted gross income minus any deductions, exemptions or other adjustments that are allowable in that tax year. Taxable income is applied to your federal and state tax brackets.

Tenancy in Common – a way for co-owners to hold title to property that allows them maximum freedom to dispose of their interests by sale, gift or will. At a co-owners death his or her share goes to beneficiaries named in a will or trust or to the legal heirs, not to the other co-owners. This is as opposed to a joint tenancy where one owner's interest automatically passes to the other owner(s) upon the first owners death.

Tenancy by the Entirety – a form of marital property ownership with a right of survivorship between spouses; very similar to a joint tenancy.

Transfer on death (TOD) – the right to name a beneficiary in a document of title which allows the beneficiary to receive the property quickly, outside of probate. Securities (stocks and bonds) can be registered in TOD form as can vehicles and real estate in certain situations. The property transferred by TOD then avoids probate.

Treasury Security – are debt obligations of the U.S. government and can be offered as bills, notes or bonds. When you buy a U.S. Treasury security, you are lending money to the federal government for a specified period of time. Since these debt obligations are backed by the "full faith and credit" of the government, they are generally considered the safest of all investments. They are viewed in the market as having virtually no "credit risk," meaning that it is highly probable your interest and principal will be paid fully and on time. This unique degree of safety results in rates of return that are generally lower than riskier debt securities.

Trust – a legal arrangement under which one person or institution (called the trustee) controls property given by another person (the grantor or trustor) for the benefit of a third person (a beneficiary). The property in the trust itself is called trust principal.

Uniform Gift to Minors Act (UGMA) – an act that allows minors to own property such as securities without an attorney setting up a special trust fund. Under the UGMA, the ownership of the funds works like it does with any other trust except that the donor must appoint a custodian (the trustee) to look after the account. The **Uniform Transfer to Minors Act (UTMA)** is like a UGMA, but allows minors to own other types of property and transfers to occur through inheritance.

Unrealized Capital Gain/Loss – profit or loss that exists on paper, resulting from any type of investment. An unrealized gain is a profitable position that has yet to be sold, such as a stock position that remains open. A gain becomes realized once the position is closed or traded for a profit. A loss becomes realized once the position is closed or traded for a loss.

Volatility – the degree of fluctuation in the value of a security, mutual fund or index. Volatility is often expressed as a mathematical measure, such as standard deviation or Beta. The greater a fund or index's volatility, the wider the fluctuation between high and low prices.

W2 Form – the IRS requires employers to report your wage and salary information on Form W-2. Your W-2 also reports the amount of federal, state and other taxes withheld from your paycheck. As an employee, the information on your W-2 is extremely important when preparing your tax return. To ensure you have it in time, the IRS requires your employer to send you a W-2 no later than January 31st following the close of the tax year, which is usually December 31st.

Whole Life Insurance – sometimes called "straight life" or "ordinary life," is a life insurance policy which is guaranteed to remain in force for the insured's entire lifetime, provided required premiums are paid, or to the maturity date. Premiums are fixed, based on the age of issue, and usually do not increase with age. The insured party normally pays premiums until death, except for limited pay policies which may be paid-up in 10 years, 20 years, or at age 65. Whole life insurance belongs to the cash value category of life insurance, because a cash value accumulates over time. This category includes universal life, variable life, and endowment policies.

Will – in estate planning, the legal document in which you state various binding intentions about what you'd like done with your property after death.

Work Credits – to receive any kind of Social Security benefit, the individual must have accumulated enough work credits. Work credits are earned through "covered employment". All work on which Social Security taxes are paid is considered covered employment. Retirement, survivor, disability and dependent benefits all require varying levels of work credits. For example, retirement benefits generally require 10 years of fully covered employment (40 work credits).

www.ingramcontent.com/pod-product-compliance
Lightning Source LLC
Chambersburg PA
CBHW080720220326
41520CB00056B/7153